Before the Chinrest

Publications of the Early Music Institute
Paul Elliott, editor

Before the Chinrest

A Violinist's Guide to the Mysteries of Pre-Chinrest Technique and Style

Stanley Ritchie

Indiana University Press
Bloomington and Indianapolis

This book is a publication of

Indiana University Press
601 North Morton Street
Bloomington, Indiana 47404–3797 USA

www.iupress.indiana.edu

Telephone orders   800-842-6796
Fax orders   812-855-7931

♾ The paper used in this publication meets the minimum requirements of the American National Standard for Information Sciences—Permanence of Paper for Printed Library Materials, ANSI Z39.48–1992.

Manufactured in the United States of America

Library of Congress Cataloging-in-Publication Data

Ritchie, Stanley.
   Before the chinrest : a violinist's guide to the mysteries of pre-chinrest technique and style / Stanley Ritchie.
     p. cm.
   Includes bibliographical references and index.
   ISBN 978-0-253-22318-0 (paperback : alkaline paper)
1. Violin—Performance—History—18th century. 2. Violin—Performance—History—17th century. I. Title.
   ML850.R57   2011
   787.2/19309   2011001028

1 2 3 4 5 17 16 15 14 13 12

To the memory of Albert Fuller,
whose passionate vision and inspiring influence
changed the course of so many lives

The Intention of Musick is not only to please the Ear, but to express Sentiments, strike the Imagination, affect the Mind, and command the Passions. The Art of playing the Violin consists in giving the Instrument a Tone that shall in a Manner rival the most perfect human Voice; and in executing every Piece with Exactness, Propriety, and Delicacy of Expression according to the true Intention of Musick.

—Francesco Geminiani

Contents

Contents

Preface and Acknowledgments

Louis Spohr (1784–1859) is credited with the invention, circa 1820, of the chinrest. The popular explanation for its introduction is that virtuoso repertoire by that time necessitated a more comfortable and secure means of supporting the violin. This opinion, however, naively overlooks the fact that the highest music ever written for the instrument had been composed seventy years earlier by Pietro Locatelli (1695–1764) in his volume of concertos entitled *L'arte del violino*! Published in 1733, the set includes a dozen caprices of extreme virtuosity, frequently requiring the performer to ascend to positions beyond the fingerboard, in at least one case to within a few centimeters of the bridge, and never resorting to the use of harmonics, as did Paganini. Personally I prefer to think that the real function of the chinrest is to protect the instrument's varnish!

Francesco Geminiani's *The Art of Playing on the Violin,* published in 1751, one of the most thorough and orderly works of its kind, is an invaluable pedagogical resource for those who aspire to revive pre-chinrest violin playing and nurture new generations of Baroque and Classical violinists. The preface, in which he describes each exercise and musical example, sheds light on the teaching methods employed in the mid-eighteenth century and, as was a custom at the time, contains much fascinating information and opinion about contemporary taste and the philosophy of music-making.

Most evident is the creativity of his teaching method: a relatively minor composer, he nonetheless managed, by means of the addition of figured bass accompaniment, to make relatively mundane and repetitious aspects of violin pedagogy interesting and enjoyable. Although apparently written for the purpose of basic instruction, since the first (and only) diagram in the book is a full-size violin fingerboard with lines or frets to indicate the position of the "white notes," he includes some quite challenging exercises, even on the first page. Perhaps modern beginning methods tend to "talk down" to children, for they seem relatively conservative and cautious in comparison with Geminiani's approach.

Whereas other books may quote Geminiani more specifically, in my teaching I use his method as a basic tool, and in this volume set down principles empirically acquired and systematically employed in almost thirty years of teaching. It is intended for use by violinists and violists already secure in their modern playing but curious to learn about technique and style as understood and practiced by their seventeenth and eighteenth-century predecessors.

Personally, in 1956, as a graduating student at the Sydney Conservatorium of Music, long before hearing about the Baroque violin, the way had been paved for me by a question in the final written examination paper: "What is meant by style in music?" It was a question that appeared annually, so that we students had ample time to reflect on the subject before sitting down to answer it, and, as a result, most of us came away from our Conservatorium training intrigued by what made Mozart different from, say, Brahms, and how one might go about creating that difference. In 1960, at the Yale School of Music, I took a course in Performance Practice and encountered for the first time the music of Heinrich von Biber: what other repertoire was there to be discovered? Previously I had known very little about the Baroque era and knew the names of but a few composers of violin music. Obviously Biber, Bach, and Corelli had not sprung up overnight like mushrooms: who, then, were their violinistic ancestors? How did it feel to be a violinist at the time of Corelli and Bach? What would it be like to play the music of these composers on the instruments with which they were familiar?

Ten years later, as a seasoned modern violinist, an innocent question led to a turning point in my career. As a member of the New York Chamber Soloists, I was a colleague of Albert Fuller, a visionary harpsichordist and teacher. One day I remarked to Albert that I was interested in learning more about Baroque music, and asked if we might read some sonatas. During our first reading session, he told me about the nascent European "Early Music" movement. At first I balked at the idea of playing on gut strings at a pitch a semitone lower than normal and using an earlier style of bow, but Albert was a very persuasive man, and soon convinced me to have one of my instruments, an eighteenth-century Tyrolean violin, returned to its original specifications. I borrowed a pre-Tourte bow and had it copied, and Albert and I began concertizing together, performing sonatas of Corelli and Bach, exploring the avenue of "authenticity." Thus began an association that resulted in 1973 in the inauguration of Aston Magna, a summer workshop and festival in Great Barrington, Massachusetts, which drew attention to Albert's determination to establish the Early Music movement as a bona fide musical endeavor in the United States.

The people initially attracted to such exploration were motivated by the common rejection of a traditional nineteenth- and twentieth-century approach to the interpretation of seventeenth- and eighteenth-century music, and the desire to find a different, more satisfying one. Having the right tool for the purpose was a solid first step, but the increasing availability of source material from which to divine the intentions of composers and the style of playing in the Baroque era opened the way to that goal. There was in the United States at the time no strictly professional motivation, so we pioneers were united solely by the enthusiasm of the explorer. Flying in the face of tradition as we were, our efforts were often regarded with skepticism and even ridicule. But gradually our numbers grew, and within a few years the movement had became firmly established. An unfortunate consequence was that some musicians who, having previously derided the concept and mocked the pioneers, now perceived that there was money to be made, and jumped aboard without paying the fare. In the cynical spirit of derision they decided that all they needed to do in order to qualify as a "Baroque" or, later, "Classical" musician, was borrow the necessary equipment. One potentially successful enterprise foundered because such players were hired by a misguided (or greedy) organizer. This book is directed, then, at those imbued with the same genuine, untainted desire to master the skills of historical performance that excited the pioneers of the Early Music movement.

My introductory words would, of course, be incomplete without expressing my gratitude to a number of people: to my many students over the years, from whom I continue to learn so much; to my doctoral student, Go Yamamoto, for his invaluable assistance in compiling the technical exercises in part 4; to my friend and colleague, Marc Destrubé, whose thorough and thoughtful criticism of the manuscript drew my attention to numerous flaws, errors, and omissions; and to Jane Behnken, Sarah Wyatt Swanson, Chandra Mevis, Angela Burton, and Rita Bernhard of Indiana University Press for their kind and patient help in seeing this project through to its conclusion.

Introduction:
How to Support the Pre-Chinrest Violin

Learning to support the violin without the aid of a chin or shoulder rest can be frustrating at first—many times I have had a modern violinist come to my studio from practicing virtuoso repertoire and say, "I feel like a beginner!"—but patient and consistent application of the following principles can result in relative comfort. Personally, as a modern violinist, having already succeeded in ridding myself of the shoulder rest and then playing Baroque violin for a few years, I discovered how little I really needed to use the chinrest!

First, it is essential that the body be as relaxed as possible. The left shoulder must remain low so that it never comes in contact with the back of the violin other than briefly when shifting down from a very high position. This is to ensure that the instrument be at all times free to vibrate naturally—to ring like a bell—and that the sound not be muted or constricted.

To help achieve this I suggest that you start by sitting down, facing directly ahead. Shoulders lowered, raise the violin straight in front of you to place it on your collarbone, which is a natural platform. In the interest of optimal relaxation of the neck and shoulders you should avoid the customary modern manner of angling the violin far to the left and looking along the fingerboard: rather, look straight ahead with the instrument at an angle of approximately 30°. The violin should rest on your collarbone, slightly tilted downward to the right, with the tailpiece beneath your left ear. In this way, should you find it necessary to use your jaw to stabilize the instrument or provide brief support, you may touch it to the tailpiece[1] instead of the top of the instrument. It also helps to have an overlapping piece of chamois attached to the button that secures the tailpiece, in order to prevent the instrument from slipping on one's clothing and also to absorb perspiration. Do not let the violin droop but instead elevate the scroll slightly above the horizontal—you will find this especially helpful in downward position changes by preventing the instrument from falling away from you. One should never grasp the neck of the violin but rather rest it on the thumb as one of three points of support, the other two being the collarbone, as described above, and—most important in the beginning stages especially—the bow. To convey this concept I use a simple image: imagine that your instrument is filled with helium and that it will float away unless you use the bow to hold it down!

Here, then, is the main reason for having the instrument more in front than to the side: in this way you are able to use the weight of the right arm, not pronation, to produce the sound. As the instrument is angled farther to the left, arm weight is proportionately reduced, and finger pressure must be applied to replace the natural, relaxed mode of tone production. Therefore keep the right elbow low, creating a sensation of hanging on the bow and transferring the weight of the arm through your index finger.

Welcome to the world of chinrestlessness!

Before the Chinrest

Part 1.

Right-Hand Technique

General Observations

Baroque and Classical music requires great subtlety of nuance and tone color and a consequent delicacy of bow control that differs in some ways from that called for in much Romantic music. There are also bow-strokes to be mastered that are especially peculiar to Baroque repertoire.[1] The transition from Baroque-style bows to the design perfected by François Tourte was gradual, and the latter was not in general use until well into the nineteenth century. The exercises that follow and the accompanying commentary are designed to acquaint you with aspects of style and right-hand technique appropriate mainly to the pre-Tourte era.

CHAPTER ONE

Tone Production

Basic Right-Hand Technique

Two words that should never, in my opinion, be used to refer to the contact between hand and bow are "hold" and "grip," as both suggest some kind of effort. Ideally, in my view, one should balance the bow in the hand as lightly as possible, exerting no physical effort. The following are exercises I prescribe to convey this concept:

Preliminary exercise: Play a down-bow on the G or D string, and lift the fingers one by one from the stick (4–3–2–1) until only the thumb remains in contact with the bow. It is essential to keep the bow moving in this exercise, which is designed to demonstrate that tone can be produced with only the weight of the bow and the motion of the hair. [*Hint: Allow the hair to rest against the outside of the thumb.*] Then, touching the bow as lightly as possible, pull and push the bow, gently raising and lowering the fingers as though they were playing notes on the stick. In this way one can experience effortless tone production, the weight of the bow producing a surprising level of sound, the hand relaxed and ready to impart the subtle nuances required in Baroque violin playing. From there I proceed with the following tone production exercises:

Exercise 1: Resting the fingers lightly on the bow, draw it very slowly at a constant speed, using the index finger to make pulsations in the sound.

Exercise 2: Use the index finger to swell the sound, increasing and decreasing the bow speed with the swell. The little finger must remain in contact with the bow to balance it and control the weight.

The Importance of Arm Weight

When playing the Baroque violin one must never resort to pronation as a means of tone production. The lower tension of gut strings, especially when the violin is tuned to A=415 or 395Hz, will not permit the use of downward pressure of the kind generated by pronation, the inward rotation of the forearm, which has the effect both of stifling the sound and frequently causing the string to give slightly and the pitch of a note to waver. One should therefore use the weight of the right arm to produce a free, resonant tone quality. To achieve this the elbow should be allowed to hang naturally,[1] with the forearm reaching upward to the plane of the bow. Avoid deliberately raising the upper arm, except when playing *flautando* or *sotto voce*.

Consider the following: when the upper arm, kept parallel to the stick, is used to transport the bow from one string to another, the natural weight of the arm is eliminated and it is then necessary to replace it by means of pronation. Something seems to be illogical in this, especially in view of the strain thereby placed upon the muscles and tendons of the upper arm—which cannot be healthy—and the tightness of the sound.

Francesco Geminiani advises that in using the bow the hand moves most, the forearm less, and the upper arm least of all.[2] One way of interpreting this is to imagine that the bow itself is leading the hand, whose job it is to adapt to the needs of the bow. This is, perhaps, the reverse of a traditional method of right-hand pedagogy in which one is taught to use each part of the arm in a particular way in order to keep the bow moving parallel to the bridge. I demonstrate to my students that if (on the E-string) the bow is allowed to slip through relaxed fingers it will fall straight downward; hence, if there is no tension in the fingers and one concentrates on *following* the bow rather than *leading* it, the bow will naturally move parallel to the bridge. This assumes, of course, that allowance be made for individual arm length, because an elbow that is advanced too far or held back will affect the direction of the bow. But it can also be a method of finding the appropriate elbow position.

The Use of Arm Weight

Here is an important exercise that demonstrates the practical use of arm weight: place the bow as close as possible to the bridge, as though you are about to play *ponticello*. Now, leaning the stick outward as you normally do, draw the bow slowly, with the hand relaxed and the elbow hanging, in such a way that you are pulling and pushing the string sideways, not pressing downward to produce the tone but directing your arm weight outward against the string. You'll find that this will enable you to play without the sound cracking but instead produce a strong, resonant tone, rich in fundamentals. The reason for this phenomenon would seem to be that when pulling the bow toward the bridge to produce the peculiar *ponticello* effect you are using less than a centimeter or two of vibrating string length, with no possibility of exciting the lower partials, whereas when directing your arm weight against the inertia of the full string length these are activated. At the same time, without vertical pressure on the string, there is no forcing of the sound, which is clear and resonant.

Please note that this is only an exercise and should not be construed as a method of tone production for constant use. The technique does, however, encourage the production of the richest, fullest tone your instrument is capable of, and, depending upon the dynamic context, it can be used at any point of contact. You'll find that because of the lower tension of the strings it's not possible to play as far from the bridge as on the modern instrument. One should never force, but rather imagine the hand as a magnet that attracts the sound from the instrument.

The low elbow is an essential component of right-hand technique on a gut-strung, low-pitched violin or viola. To avoid confusion later on, note that I make frequent reference throughout the book to "raising" the elbow or forearm or arm when describing certain lifted or lightened strokes. This does not negate the basic concept, for even when one raises the arm, the relationship of elbow to wrist and hand should always be the same—the elbow should always be relatively low, with minimal tension in the upper arm.

CHAPTER TWO

Bow-Strokes

The term "bow-stroke" has different connotations according to the context. In its simple form it defines the various ways in which the bow can be used: *détaché, sautillé, legato, martelé,* and so on. It can also refer, however, to the passage of the bow across the string or to the way in which a particular player uses the bow. To avoid confusion, therefore, I shall use the word "gesture" to describe what happens when a number of consecutive bow-strokes occur.

For me a bow-stroke of any kind is the motion of the arm through the air; that one has a bow in one's hand, and what results when the bow comes in contact with the string, are secondary. Indeed, in my teaching I will at times prescribe the following preliminary exercise: first sing a phrase silently, then without the bow make an imaginary bow-stroke, with the arm and hand moving appropriately to fit the dynamic shape and nuances you have in mind, and string crossings as needed. Then, with bow in hand, replicate the arm gestures so as to play the phrase as you imagined it. This is one example of what I term the "choreography" of bowing.

If I ask a student to assume a position of readiness to play, I want to see what he or she does with the right arm. Sometimes the student places the bow on the string, but this is an incorrect posture: correctly, the bow should be suspended about half an inch above the string in anticipation of the first stroke.[1] It is also to this position that the bow should return upon completion of the stroke or gesture.

Lifted Strokes

Essentially there is no difference between the basic stroke used in playing separate *legato* notes and that for notes that require the bow to be lifted from the string. For instance, when playing short eighth-notes at a fast tempo, the arm should move back and forth in a fluid motion: there should be no active use of the fingers other than those of transmitting the weight of the arm and balancing the bow. To shorten the notes, one need only allow the bow to rise from the string by raising the arm slightly and using the fourth finger to take the weight. Note that the transition from the long note to the short is *legato* and that the bow should rise only after the short note.

As an exercise, in the lower half of the bow, start by playing repeated eighth-notes *legato* with loose wrist and hand. Then, without changing tempo, hesitating, or altering the motion of the arm, allow the bow to rise occasionally from the string. For example:

Then try reversing the process, so that you begin the exercise with a lifted stroke and randomly lower the elbow to create a longer articulation:

Here is a passage from Bach's C-major *Fuga* that requires the alternation of longer and shorter bow-strokes:

The purpose, then, of this kind of bowing is to give more melodic value to certain notes so that they stand out from the rest of the texture or, conversely, that the shorter notes retreat.

Slurred Notes

Articulations of two or more slurred notes require special attention according to the context in which they occur. Here is a typical passage:

Each pair of notes must be played with a *diminuendo* and a delicate lightening or lift of the bow. The balancing function of the fourth finger is the key to successful execution of this and similar strokes—at the end of each pair the pressure of the finger must be increased to reduce the amount of arm weight. This particular example would usually be played in the lower half of the bow where it rises more easily from the string, but the illustration can be performed in any part of the bow depending on the desired degree of articulation. I have chosen leaping thirds to demonstrate the point, and these are normally played in a more energetic or lively way than those in a passage such as the following, which are usually played in the upper part of the bow, although a "tempo" indication such as *vivace* might suggest a stronger dynamic or degree of articulation.

The style described here, whereby slurred notes will be played with a slight *diminuendo,* is also applicable to groups of three, four, six, or even eight notes. (Below, in the section "Swift-Bows," I talk about "combination strokes," in which slurred notes and separate notes occur in repeated patterns.) As for dynamic shading, the rule about playing slurred notes with a *diminuendo* is true until such time as the shape of the notes in a group changes from the simple diatonic. Obviously a passage such as the following in Bach's D-minor *Allemanda* has a more complex dynamic shape!

Retaking

The so-called hook-stroke is generally inappropriate in Baroque music, not only because stopping the bow stifles the natural resonance of the instrument but also because of its tendency to cause a stiff predictability in an otherwise lyrical musical line. However, energetically articulated passages in dotted rhythms, which occur frequently, require a lifted stroke that involves retaking the bow. Here is a useful basic exercise: in the lower half of the bow, in one curving motion, draw a swift down-bow, returning through the air to the point at which you started:

Then repeat this stroke several times without stopping or changing its speed until you return to the frog at the fermata. Be sure to keep wrist and fingers relaxed:

Next, repeat the exercise, executing it in one swift motion—but this time collide with the string close to the frog, as if by accident:

Now join the groups together:

Now you should practice long chains of retaken notes. Once you're comfortable with the stroke, start using it in "five-finger exercises" on one string, and then in simple scales. Remember always to execute the stroke in one constant, smooth, swift motion:

Z-Bowing

This is a name given to a stroke frequently employed in Baroque music, where a passage in dotted rhythm needs to be played *legato* rather than lifted. The complex technique involved in its execution requires a relaxed elbow and a loose wrist, and is a combination of a continuous motion of the forearm and a flicking action of the hand.

In the down-bow version, during each of the dotted notes the hand must fall slightly faster than the bow and be flicked upward again for each of the short notes. In the up-bow version the opposite action is used: during the dotted note, allow the hand to rise slightly faster than the arm and then flick it downward to rejoin the forearm. In both versions, above all, one must maintain the smooth motion of the forearm, using only the hand to create the short notes.

To practice this stroke, begin without using the bow: imagine that you are plucking something swiftly from a table, flicking the hand upward without moving the forearm. Then, on an open string, first play a continuous, slow down-bow, focusing your attention on the sensation of the descent of the forearm. Then repeat the stroke, this time flicking the hand upward without disturbing the smooth descent of the forearm.

To practice the stroke in an up-bow, imagine that you are trying to shake something off your hand, flicking it downward. Then, as with the down-bow, first play a long, sustained up-bow on an open string and repeat it while flicking the hand:

When you are comfortable performing the stroke on an open string, proceed to play a simple "five-finger exercise" several times, focusing on smooth forearm motion:

Then, without hesitation, switch to the Z-bowing version:

Bach's D-minor *Corrente* contains a number of passages that call for Z-bowing:

In this case the up-bow on the first note in the second measure brings the bow to the frog, and the following two bars, when executed with Z-bowing, bring the bow to the point, where it needs to be for what follows. All similar passages in this movement should be bowed the same way. The hook-stroke, which is a type of *martelé,* should rarely be used, normally not for more than a few notes, and definitely not in this passage.

An important variation of this technique, which is used in many situations in the Baroque repertoire, involves playing a long note followed by shorter notes and returning to the frog to play another long note without accenting the note before the bar line. Practice the following exercises so as to have the sensation of making a constant up-Z-bow. Raising your arm slightly to avoid accenting the first eighth-note, gradually work your way back to the frog:

Remember that the note that follows a dot or a suspension is to be played lightly.

Martelé and *Spiccato*

Neither of these bow-strokes is applicable in Baroque performance nor, for that matter, in Classical music. Quite apart from being historically inappropriate—in the case of *martelé* the stroke is certainly intended for use with a Tourte-style bow, and it is recorded that *spiccato* was first experimented with in Vienna in the late years of the eighteenth century, regarded as a fad, and soon rejected—neither of these strokes works well with a Baroque bow. Furthermore, a better effect can be achieved by the use of other strokes.

I tell my students that the Baroque bow never stops moving until you put it back in the case. By this I mean, simply, that the right arm must always be fluid in motion, that one should always make use of the kind of "follow-through" that a golfer or tennis player utilizes in any stroke. Indeed, there is a very good physiological reason for this: just as the follow-through in sports prevents injury that could result from an abrupt cessation of motion, so it is with the string player's right arm: the use of a stroke that requires a sudden freezing of motion can eventually cause injury. Short sounds can be produced on the violin without the jarring motion of the *martelé,* usually with lifted strokes, but even *staccato* strokes at the point of the bow do not require a sudden stop of the forearm's motion and can be completed with a "follow-through."

From the musical point of view any stroke that inhibits the instrument's natural resonance is really a special effect and should be used sparingly. For this reason the hook-stroke, a variation of *martelé,* is generally not appropriate in Baroque music because of its tendency to stifle the resonance of the sound. Unless a special effect of the kind is called for, it is preferable to lift the bow slightly.

When a passage calls for short notes that sound better played on the string in the upper half of the bow one must use the fourth finger to balance the bow and lighten each stroke, releasing the pressure of the first finger. Once again, be sure to use a fluid, constant arm motion, never stopping the bow between notes. One example is the subject of Bach's G-minor *Fugue* (which is best bowed "as it comes," even in reverse):

Example XX in *The Art of Playing on the Violin* is an invaluable source of information regarding what one may assume to be the Corelli school of technique and expression as transmitted by Geminiani. He provides a list of notes of decreasing value, each with different bowing styles—swelled, uninflected *detaché, staccato,* or slurred—labeling them *buono* (good), *cattivo* (bad), *particolare* (special effect), *meglio* (better), *ottimo* (the best), or *pessimo* (the worst). They are grouped, furthermore, in two categories of tempo: *Adagio* or *Andante,* and *Allegro* or *Presto.* It is worth noting, for example, that sixteenth-notes with uninflected *detaché* are classified as *cattivo* when played slowly but as *buono* when played rapidly (our *sautillé*). On the other hand, sixteenth-notes played in a rapid tempo with a lifted stroke (our *spiccato*) are considered to be *cattivo,* and eighth-notes played with an uninflected *detaché* are dismissed as *pessimo*!

These categorizations give us, accustomed as we are to playing with the Tourte-style bow, an important insight into the eighteenth-century musicians' understanding of pre-Tourte bow-strokes and tasteful expression in the Italian style; Example XX, therefore, is an indispensable aid to modern-trained musicians wishing to approximate their way of playing.

Spiccato, the term used in string playing to refer to a stroke produced by the rapid vertical motion of the hand, literally means "distinct," and one finds the word frequently in Baroque music, often in strange-sounding combinations such as *"Largo e spiccato."* *Spiccato,* the bow-stroke, has no use in Baroque music and is much misused in Classical music. The appropriate stroke for clearly articulated 16th-note passagework is *sautillé.*

Sautillé

To practice *sautillé,* begin by drawing the bow slowly back and forth on an open string, watching the frog or tip of the bow to be sure the stroke is continuously lateral. Then gradually move the bow faster and shorten the stroke until rapid, clear notes result, with the hair never leaving the string. When executing this stroke in the middle of the bow the stick tends to rise and lift the hair from the string, and the harder you press on the bow, the more it tries to do so. One may vary the degree of articulation according to the mood of the passage by playing further toward the point, where the notes will be less clear; however, the closer to the middle of the bow one plays, the clearer and more *"spiccato"* the effect will be. Most significantly, however, *allegro* sixteenth-notes should be played on the string, not off. This instruction is in accordance with that of Bismantova, who says that *passaggi* (fast notes) should be played "with short strokes at the point of the bow."[2]

Bariolage

This is a term that refers to a rapid stroke, usually notated in sixteenth-notes, in which the bow passes back and forth between two strings, specifically when an open string is repeated. One frequently encounters such passages in the music of Vivaldi and Bach, and often one note is held as a pedal tone. Here is a familiar example in Bach's E-major *Preludio:*

Obviously it is important in such a passage to bring out the moving voice and underplay the pedal tone; the following is an exercise I prescribe:

Each eighth-note should be played strongly, with pressure by the index finger, and the sixteenth-notes released and played lightly, the pairs of notes grouped as triplets, long-short, long-short. Focus also on pulling the down-bow in a lateral direction, not circular, pivoting around the elbow, which should remain low, the upper arm relaxed. (As I have remarked elsewhere, here again each pair of notes constitutes one bow-stroke.) Having practiced the exercise slowly for a while, play the passage up to the desired tempo, and you'll find that whereas it will no longer be possible to play it in triplets, the melodic voice will now stand out easily from the texture.

This practice method can be applied to all similar passages. Occasionally one will encounter one such as this, in the finale of Bach's C-major *Sonata,* in which the bowing is reversed:

Once again, practice the *bariolage* in triplets, remembering to keep the elbow low and the upper arm relaxed and neutral.

Sometimes this type of bowing occurs over three strings. This famous passage in Bach's E-major *Preludio,* an arpeggiated *bariolage,* requires a complex, continuous arm motion:

It is most important *not* to think of each string as one plays this passage but rather to concentrate on the arm motions involved: a lateral movement of the forearm to produce the sound and a vertical one to change the plane of the bow. One important piece of advice: *Don't try to play each string individually*! In order to arrive at a comfortable, consistent execution, one must focus solely on achieving a smooth, involuntary, arpeggiated bow-stroke, and, to do so, it is best to practice at first on open strings.

Here is a preparatory exercise:

Practice it as follows: With the elbow hanging loosely, use an upward and downward motion of the forearm to catch the E and D. Repeat the first measure until the action is involuntary, and then go to the subsequent measures and work on each in the same way. The basic purpose of this exercise is to accustom you to using your forearm instead of your upper arm for the string crossings. The elbow will rise and fall, but although it is essential that the upper arm not be constricted, neither must it initiate the action.

Another exercise cannot be notated, as it requires random motion: start by playing rapid repeated sixteenth-notes on the open A-string, and then, without interrupting the repetition, randomly raise and lower your forearm, gradually reducing the number of notes on each string. Continue in this manner, working to achieve the smooth vertical arm motion that results in your being able to play each string only once. At first this will sound chaotic, but the object is to arrive at a fluid execution of the pattern of string crossing required. Just remember:

$$\begin{array}{c} \uparrow \\ \leftarrow \quad \rightarrow \\ \downarrow \end{array}$$

These two motions combined are the secret of the smooth execution of this passage.

Ondeggiando

This word means, literally, "making waves" and refers to a *legato* stroke between two strings that can apply to as few as two notes or as many as sixteen. It requires the use of a free, relaxed wrist so as to allow the hand to make a gentle, vertical waving motion while the forearm moves smoothly up and down. Most important in general, and especially when there is a pedal tone, is that the pedal tone be unaccented and that the change from one string to the other be slightly blurred, with a brief, virtually inaudible double-stop. It could be notated as follows:

For an exercise, commence by playing a plain open-string fifth a few times and then, with the elbow low, change to a vertical waving motion (*it is important to execute the stroke, wrist relaxed and flexible, by raising the hand, not lowering it*):

The following passage in Bach's *Ciaccona* is a fine example of the *ondeggiando* style:

CHAPTER THREE

Chordal Technique

In 1933, in an article in the *Musical Times*, Albert Schweitzer promoted the idea, originally conceived by musicologist Arnold Schering at the beginning of the twentieth century, that there had once been a bow that could play chords in the Bach solo sonatas and partitas with all the notes sustained. This prompted violinist Emil Telmányi to invent what became known as the "Vega" bow, whose frog was hinged to enable the player to slacken the hair when playing double-stops and chords, and to tighten it with thumb pressure when playing a single line. Recordings made using this device are notable for the way that each chord stands out from the texture. Without commenting further on the effect this produces, I shall simply point out that there is no historical evidence to support the existence of such a bow. Schweitzer, an organist, apparently conceived of chords literally, without arpeggiation; however, as string players, we should be thinking of them in the way a lutenist might, and, in polyphonic passages, always playing *horizontally,* not vertically.

A number of principles must be kept in mind when playing chords in the Baroque style. But first I offer some suggestions concerning the basic right-hand technique of chord playing:

1. Always keep your elbow low—let the arm hang loosely.
2. The fingers should be relaxed: it is essential for the production of a full, resonant, and unforced tone that the bow be supported loosely.
3. Never start a chord on the string but come from the air at an oblique angle.
4. Never "put" the bow on the lowest string by raising your arm but rather allow the bow to fall there by relaxing the pressure of the fourth finger. You'll find that this produces a firm yet unforced bass-note for the chord.
5. The fingers should always point away from the direction of the stroke: when playing a down-bow chord let the wrist lead and the fingers trail behind.
6. When playing a chord down-bow, the stroke should be generated by allowing the elbow to fall, with the forearm and hand following.
7. When playing an up-bow chord, make the stroke by letting the forearm fall toward your ribs.
8. Be sure that the upper arm follows in the direction that the bow, hand, and forearm have taken but that it does not lead—never raise it to place the bow on the bass-note.

The normal way to play a chord in Baroque style involves a greater or lesser degree of arpeggiation, depending upon the context. The type of "breaking" of a chord such as one finds in the opening allegro of the Max Bruch G-minor *Concerto* is inappropriate in Baroque music, as are a couple of other methods. In my teaching I have given nicknames to these three ways of breaking chords:

The first I call "ta-WHA!"

as in:

The second, "ha-CHOO!"

as in:

And the third, which is a combination of the other two, "ta-wha-CHOO!"

as in the continuation of the previous passage:

Notice that I have chosen examples from Bach's unaccompanied music to make my point, and I have done so for a particular reason that I shall touch on here without delving more deeply into the subject of Bach interpretation: there is, in essence, no such thing as "unaccompanied" music. When you play a chord in an unaccompanied piece, you are providing your own bass line, and therefore your own accompaniment. The bottom note of a chord must be on the beat, for it *is* the "beat." Imagine—if you can—what it would be like to play with a continuo player who always anticipated the beat in the left hand!

In compositions with figured bass accompaniment, one does at times find examples of chords that would seem to ignore this rule, such as this from Jean-Marie Leclair's *Sonata in C Minor*, op. 5, no. 6, known as *Le tombeau*:

Even the first chord, with descending grace notes that are rolled downward and then up again, does not break the rule of starting on the beat, because the first note of the measure, the E-natural, must be placed precisely on the downbeat.[1] The bottom note of the second chord, however, must be played on the beat, after which the chord is rolled upward through the grace notes to the D-flat.

One should remember when performing chords in Baroque music that each one is comprised of two or three individual double-stops. When a four-note chord is played as a "ta-WHA!" only the outer double-stops are heard—the middle one is ignored. In principle, then, the appropriate way to play chords in Baroque and much Classical music is to roll them upward from the bass-note, the degree of arpeggiation dictated by affect, tempo, dynamic, and function in the overall context. Certainly there are times when a chord needs to be percussive or crisply played with little noticeable arpeggiation, but the styles of breaking described above are rarely, if ever, appropriate.

Context will dictate whether one should start rolling a chord from a single note or from a double-stop, and the speed of rolling, too. In a particularly soft or tender moment one may roll a chord slowly and gently, as a lute player or harpsichordist might. If there is a particularly interesting harmonic shift or melodic twist it may also be effective to linger briefly on one of the notes. In a declamatory or *vivace* passage a rapid arpeggiation will usually be appropriate.

When playing polyphonic music it is possible also to "shade" a chord in such a way as to allow one note to stand out more than the others. If, for instance, one needs to emphasize the bass-note, a vertical diminuendo is required; if the tenor is the predominant line, one should use the weight of the arm to lean more on the D-string.

Chords may be played either down-bow or up-bow at any dynamic level. In an accompanied recitative in a Mozart opera, for example, off-beat triads are best played up-bow, for in that way there is no hard edge to the sound. A succession of chords should normally be played "as they come"—reserve the "down, down, down" for places where the music calls for a percussive, extremely energetic or angry effect.

Finally, the ideal effect in chord playing will be achieved by having the sensation that one is falling through the strings, not going around the outside of them. One is more likely to achieve this with the hand relaxed and the palm soft, so that the work is being done by arm weight, not finger pressure. Most important, one should never use the upper arm to make the stroke, but let the elbow hang.

One way to acquire this technique is to start by playing a simple *legato arpeggio*, drawing the bow smoothly over the strings with relaxed hand and wrist, allowing the arm to fall in a fluid motion:

Then gradually blur the arpeggiation so that the bow touches each string and pair of strings briefly as you lower your arm. Avoid any kind of angularity, focusing your attention on the smooth descent of the elbow. Rather than planning when you're going to arrive on each string, be surprised when you do:

Hint: Now that you know the notes, which look so angular, close your eyes and focus instead on the sensation of the smooth falling and rising of your arm.

Don't overlook the fact that you need to play chords up-bow as well. What you must feel this time is the smooth motion of the forearm swinging outward away from the body during the down-bow, and inward toward the ribs for the up-bow:

Here is another simple exercise: placing the bow on the E-string slightly above the frog, relax and curve your fourth finger to allow the point of the bow to fall until the hair comes to rest on the G-string. Keep your wrist loose, and the weight of the bow will cause it to straighten. First, do this a few times without allowing the elbow to rise, and then, as the bow contacts the G-string, draw a down-bow with the wrist still flat and the relaxed fingers left behind. You will notice that the tone produced in this way is full and resonant.[2]

This technique may be used to good effect in the opening of the *Allemanda* of Bach's B-minor *Partita:*

When playing such a passage, always keep your arm on the plane of the melodic voice and your hand relaxed. By releasing the pressure of the fourth finger to allow the bow to fall to the lowest string under its own weight, the bass-notes stand out clearly and the chord is produced with far less effort than when raising the elbow. Both the tone quality and the clarity of the polyphony will be enhanced when the melody is resumed.

CHAPTER FOUR

Bow Division

"Choreography" is a comprehensive term that I use in my teaching to describe the artful use of bow-strokes to shape a musical phrase. According to Michael Vernon, director of the Ballet Department at the Indiana University Jacobs School of Music, choreography is "the art and craft of marrying steps and movements to music in such a way that the music is illuminated and the combination of music and movement produces an emotion in the spectator that is satisfying and expressively cohesive." Just as in ballet, then, where the choreographer combines steps and gestures to tell a story or depict an emotion, so the string player, when interpreting music, must use the bow in a variety of ways to "illuminate" the musical line, to evoke an emotional picture and realize the architecture of the piece.

Beyond the purely mechanical in basic violin technique, then, skillful interpretation requires great subtlety in bowing, whose ingredients include speed and point of contact as well as attack and pressure. It is not enough merely to know how to pull and push the bow across the strings, but in so doing how to produce a sound of appropriate volume and color at any point in a phrase or gesture, and how to shape individual notes artistically.

It seems to me to be habitual nowadays for many string players, whether inadvertently or deliberately, to use a whole bow wherever possible, necessary or not. One common fault among Baroque violinists, then, is what I refer to as the "violin-thing." This is what occurs when a player, not thinking ahead, uses too rapid a bow-stroke on a long note, arriving so soon in the upper third of the bow as to be incapable of sustaining or swelling the sound. For example, a dotted note in an *Adagio* or an *Andante* will often need to be played with a *crescendo* because of the progression toward a dissonance on the dot, or else to be sustained and shaped to create a *cantabile* effect: both of these are thereby made impossible. Another related fault is to play an *appoggiatura* and its resolution in such as way as to render the resolution inaudible, once again because the bow has been drawn too swiftly and too much of it wasted on the *appoggiatura*. One must carefully calculate the speed and amount of bow required to achieve every effect.

An exercise I recommend to correct these tendencies is simple but effective. Using white chalk or narrow strips of adhesive paper, divide the bow into four equal parts. Then, passing the bow over the strings always at the same, even speed, practice each of the first two intonation exercises (Part 4, Chapter 14) in these ways, using a quarter of the bow for each note. In numbers 4 and 5 the bow direction will reverse every two measures. It is essential that the bow speed remain constant and that you maintain firm contact between bow and string:

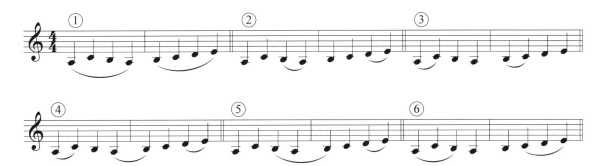

Another version of this exercise is simply to put one mark in the middle of the bow and, in any of the exercises (four notes to a bow) be sure to arrive at that point precisely when the third note is played.

These are only half a dozen samples of the kind of exercise that will result in disciplined control over the amount of bow used in any stroke. Improvise some of your own, and use the same technique when working on each of the other intonation exercises. One of the results of the efficient use of these exercises is the development of technical serenity—each hand working in as economical and fluid a way as possible. Strive to achieve this, for tension or awkwardness in either hand or arm will impede the efficiency of the other. The ultimate goal of all technical practice is a state of unawareness of anything but the music and its expression, as though the instrument is a part of your body: the bow your breath, the violin your larynx.

CHAPTER FIVE

Swift-Bows

Here are two exercises that are very useful for developing the ability to pass lightly and rapidly from one end of the bow to the other. This is an invaluable skill in Baroque interpretation: one often encounters a passage in which a light, unaccented up-bow is necessary, as well as gestures requiring a strong but unforced down-bow.

As I have observed earlier, I define "bow-stroke" simply as the passage of the arm through the air. In the following exercise the complete bow-stroke starts and finishes at the frog:

Practice this exercise playing the quarter-note at the point, turning the corner without accenting it and then returning to the frog through the air, the bow lifted from the string by the pressure of the fourth finger and the elevation of the wrist. To perform this stroke correctly one must elevate the right elbow slightly on the up-bow in order to reduce the weight. *It is most important that the arm not return on the same plane.* The soft quarter-note should not be played as an upbeat but as though it belongs to the previous dotted half.

A typical gesture in which this technique must be used is the following cadential formula in Bach's G-minor *Adagio:*

The anticipatory note, D, which in such a case is not to be treated as an up-beat, must be connected to the dotted eighth and played very lightly, forearm raised and bow balanced by the fourth finger, which causes the bow to lift slightly before the octave:

I tell my students to fit the words "going home" to this gesture.

The next exercise focuses on the lifted down-bow, which is used frequently both on single notes and on double-stops or chords. It may be found in a context that requires a rapid, dramatic stroke, or one that merely needs a clear articulation before the next note:

When executing this stroke use the weight of the arm to produce the *forte* quarter-note, taking care to keep the hand relaxed: the little finger must support the weight of the stick, with the forearm slightly elevated to raise the hair from the string. The little finger's function of balancing the bow now comes into play when the hair once more contacts the string in the *piano* up-bow. The forearm remains elevated throughout the dotted half-note, and the bow lifts at the end of the completed bow-stroke. Here is an excerpt from Bach's E-major *Bourée* that requires this stroke:

In the *Sarabanda* of Bach's B-minor *Partita* a gently lifted down-bow slightly detaches the first chord from the second in order to convey the dance's lilting charac-ter. Note also the lift of the bow after the *mordent*-like figure in the fifth bar:

In the *Tempo di Borea,* however, each down-bow chord in the first two measures requires a strong attack, and a lift before the following quarter-note; in my rendition of this excerpt, the *staccato* dots suggest short but lighter strokes:

In a piece in triple metre, such as a simple Minuet, one should play the third quarter-note lightly, with a gently lifted stroke, so that the passage sounds like this:

However, in order to play the same passage elegantly with the second and third notes slurred, the first quarter-note must be lifted:

Since the example I have given is Minuet-like, I should point out that the assumed tempo would be *allegro*. In a slower tempo, where the affect is more tranquil, similar nuances should be applied but with subtler lifting or lightening of the bow. In truly *cantabile* passages, articulations may be barely discernable, but it is important to remember that our instrument is imitating the human voice and speech, and that articulation is every bit as important for the clarity of instrumental music as it is when we speak or sing.

CHAPTER SIX

Combination Strokes

A characteristic style of Baroque articulation is one in which slurred and separate articulations occur. In such cases the swift-bow techniques described above come into play:

The first pattern should be played in the lower half, where, on each retake, with the
forearm raised so as to suspend it, the bow will rise easily from the string. The second
will feel more comfortable in the upper half.

Each one, though, can be played with a "walking" bow-stroke, using the Z-bowing technique described earlier. This will result in, and should be used for, a subtler,
less energetic affect. Obviously, then, the first pattern will start in the lower half and
work its way down to the point and the second will "walk up" from point to frog:

A useful exercise is to join the two together thus, walking from one end of the
bow to the other and back, but still taking care to observe the nuances indicated:

I must distinguish here between situations in which normal alternation of bow
direction is indicated and those that call for a double down-bow, as in certain dance
movements. The following passage from a trio sonata by Biber, for example, is a
dance tune whose sprightly energy suggests retaking the bow in order to give the
notes equal emphasis:

In this passage the quarter-notes should be played in the lower half of the bow, clearly
lifted, and the eighths on the string.

Part 2.

Left-Hand Technique

CHAPTER SEVEN

Position-Changing Exercises

Basic Concepts

Position refers not to the hand but to the arm. Hence "First-position" is that configuration of the arm that allows the fingers to fall naturally, without extension or contraction, on all the notes between G-sharp on the G-string and B-natural on the E-string.

Position-changing or Shifting refers to the motion made by the left arm in conveying the hand up or down the fingerboard.

The Swing: This is the term I use to describe and refer to a lateral motion of the left arm whose principal purpose is to maintain a balanced left-hand position. It is also an essential element of shifting technique.

The Position of the Left Hand

In order to find an ideal basic left-hand position, imagine that your hand is a quadruped and that you must distribute the weight of the hand equally among the four fingers. As a basic exercise, place the fingers on the E-string in first-position—F-sharp, G-sharp, A, B—elevating the hand slightly so that the fingers are curved down to the string in a natural way, neither extended nor overbalanced. Take a moment to notice where the elbow is when you do this.

Now, without altering the finger pattern raise the fingers slightly, in unison, and move the elbow slightly toward your body so that your fingers are poised above the A-string. Drop them in unison on B, C-sharp, D, and E. Repeat the procedure for the D and G-string as well. When this is done correctly, a line from the point of the elbow to the space between the second and third fingers will remain absolutely straight.

The Swing

This is a term I have coined to describe a motion of the left arm that is essential to shifting technique as well as to the simple passage of the hand from one string-plane to another. Its purpose is to maintain the balance of the hand and the shape of the fingers as they rise and fall and to help avoid unnecessary contortion, extension, and contraction.

As mentioned above, my definition of "position" is that configuration of the left arm that permits the fingers to fall naturally and accurately on the notes. I believe that, to the extent possible for each individual hand, it is important to maintain the curved shape of the fingers as they fall to the string and rise from it, using the third joint as a hinge in an action much akin to that of piano hammers.

As an exercise to illustrate this point, play a simple G-major two-octave scale in first position, from G to B and back. Be careful, however, not to change the shape of the fingers, neither stretching to reach the notes on the G-string nor contracting them as you rise to the E-string, but rather moving the elbow out from the body as you ascend and then back again under the violin as you return. Imagine a line from the point of the elbow to the space between the second and third fingers, and be sure to keep it straight as you play the scale, above all never letting the arm bend sideways at the wrist. The motion your arm makes during this exercise, which I refer to as "The Swing," causes your hand to pivot around the neck of the instrument while allowing your fingers to remain as relaxed as possible.

The Swing is also an essential ingredient in position-changing technique. Ideally the focus of your attention in the execution of a shift will be the arm, not the fingers, for it is the task of the arm to transport the fingers (whose principal function is changing the vibrating length of the string) from one part of the fingerboard to another. This motion may be lateral or lengthwise or a combination of both: swinging the arm inward when shifting draws the hand up the fingerboard, and swinging it outward draws the hand down. The amount of swing necessary will depend, of course, on the distance to be traveled in shifting and whether string crossing is also involved.

The ultimate goal in left-hand technique is to be unaware of the process: to be able to forget the left side of your body in order to be able to focus all your attention on expression, which is the principal function of your right arm. Strive, then, in your technical practice, to use the bow firmly to aid in the relaxation of the left side of your body, always "supporting" the instrument with it, even imagining that it is pushing and pulling the left hand up and down during position changes. Have the sensation that the two arms are working together to cause position changes to occur: this will help you to relax and feel comfortable in their execution, and consequently to play with consistent accuracy.

Shifting

The normal modern-violin method of shifting, especially downward, should not be used on the Baroque violin. It is certainly possible to shift upward in the modern way—moving fingers and thumb together—but not as satisfactory from an aesthetic point of view. In order to avoid clutching the instrument between chin and shoulder, thereby creating undesirable tension in the neck and shoulder muscles and having a muffling effect on the tone, one must learn to use the thumb to support the violin and, when shifting, as a fulcrum around which the hand pivots, and a constant point of reference for the fingers. When changing position without a chinrest one must prepare by advancing the thumb as far as necessary, and then the wrist, so that the forearm is in the new position; execute the shift by swinging the elbow inward to move up and outward to move down. The distance of the shift—first position to second, or to third or fourth, and so on, will determine the degree of preparation and swing needed to complete the action smoothly. Obviously, when shifting, the side of the hand must touch the neck of the violin lightly, if at all. Carefully calculate the distance the fore-arm should be moved in anticipation: once the thumb and arm are in place, the fingers need only to move as a unit—without extension or contraction—to rejoin the forearm in a natural and relaxed shape.

Example 1c in Geminiani's *The Art of Playing on the Violin,* which shows all possible fingerings for notes up to the seventh position, provides excellent material for a basic shifting exercise. In the following exercises, based on Geminiani's example, it is important to keep the first finger down at all times, and when playing the whole-tones to leave each finger down until descending. Take care to assume a balanced hand position, with the arm far enough under the violin to permit the fingers to fall from directly above the notes. If the notes are in tune, the arm is in the correct position.[1]

Here are exercises with which to practice shifting technique. In each exercise make sure that your fingers are articulating the notes clearly, that you are not clutching the neck of the violin, and that the thumb and wrist are prepared for the shift. In preparation for the descending shift, elevate the hand slightly so that the fingers will fall in the normal balanced configuration. Finally, it is essential that the first finger never leave the string.

Exercise A: Place the thumb opposite the second finger with the wrist bent slightly toward the body of the violin and repeat the notes in the first measure until you're playing them automatically, involuntarily, and rapidly. Then, without hesitating or thinking about the fingers, switch abruptly to the next measure, using The Swing to change position, pivoting around the thumb. Repeat the exercise several times. Note that you must be thinking of the intervals and not be confused by the change of key!

Exercise B: With the arm in third position and the thumb pointed backward under the neck, play the notes in the first measure, repeating them until you're playing them automatically. While playing them move your forearm into first position—the wrist advanced, the elbow slightly to the left. Then, suddenly, without moving the thumb or the arm again, allow your hand to fly back and rejoin the forearm in first position.

Exercise C: Now put the two previous exercises together. In first position, with the thumb opposite the second finger, repeat the notes in the first measure until they become automatic. (The joint at the base of your first finger must be touching the neck very lightly!) Then, without interrupting the fingering pattern, in one fluid motion swing your arm up to third position. Repeat the procedure in third position and then swing back to first. To execute this maneuver successfully, you must make sure that your shoulder and wrist are relaxed and, above all, elevate your violin and let your left shoulder hang, staying well away from the back of the instrument.

The thumb should remain in one place, with the hand pivoting around it and the forearm anticipating each shift. Eventually you'll find that you can play the complete group of notes back and forth without stopping and with complete relaxation.

Here is another exercise that requires the thumb to be placed opposite the second finger. To shift to third position in this scale, merely swing the elbow inward so that the hand pivots around the thumb. You'll find that there's no sensation of changing position: indeed, the motion can be likened to walking up the fingerboard as opposed to hopping, which is analogous to what happens when the thumb and the fingers move together:

Now practice descending. Here is a preliminary exercise:

At the fermata, prepare for the shift by arching the wrist backward so that the forearm arrives in first position with the thumb pointed backward and the base of the first finger barely touching the neck, if at all. Then suddenly release the hand to fly lightly back and rejoin the forearm in the natural configuration. It is important that the forearm, having already arrived in first position, not move any further.

Now, using this technique, do the following exercise in the same way that you practiced the ascending figure, repeating the first measure several times before abruptly changing to the second:

Now play the scale itself. Begin by placing all four fingers on the string, stopping the D/A fifth with the first finger. With the thumb pointed backward under the neck, quickly run down from third position to first:

Finally, put the two scales together: place the thumb opposite the second finger and use the arm to pivot around it, swinging inward as you ascend and outward as you descend. Aim to execute each scale in a single smooth motion: when you can do this you will find that you have no sensation of shifting.

Half-Position

When playing the music of Bach, one frequently encounters passages that require the use of half-position. Here are some exercises to help you become more comfortable with its use. Be sure to sustain the fingers on the string for as long as indicated:

Vibrato

A particular type of vibrato that I find most useful in Baroque repertoire is vertical, which is created by subtly changing the amount of finger pressure on the string.[2] Here is a basic exercise to be practiced without the bow:

Placing a finger gently on the string as though you were playing a harmonic, slowly and deliberately press the string down to the fingerboard, then relax the pressure without losing contact with the string. Repeat this rhythmically, slowly at first, and then gradually faster, raising the finger less and less until it remains in constant contact with the fingerboard.

When applied to a bowed note, the effect is a subtle warming of the sound without noticeable variation of pitch. One can, of course, if one wishes, allow this vertical squeezing and releasing motion to mutate into the normal oscillation of hand vibrato.

Part 3.

Interpretation

CHAPTER EIGHT

Expression

If there is one clue that should help us understand the rarity of dynamics and other indications of expression in much of the music composed before the end of the eighteenth century or the beginning of the nineteenth, it is that musicians of the period were provided with a set of basic rules of interpretation that simplified their professional life. Francesco Geminiani's treatise lays out many of these, as do those of Carl Philipp Emanuel Bach, Leopold Mozart, and Daniel Gottlob Türk. Indeed, even the terms *crescendo* and *decrescendo* or *diminuendo* are rare until well into the nineteenth century, other than where it would not be normal to use them. One may find the word *crescendo* on groups of slurred notes, which, according to Leopold Mozart, should normally fall away dynamically, but *decrescendo* hardly ever. For example, in the entire orchestral score of Beethoven's first piano concerto only one *decrescendo* is indicated, and that occurs in the twelve measures of string accompaniment leading to the coda of the finale, which start *pianissimo* and get progressively softer!

But the didactic literature of the period provides guidelines for the perception of expressive clues, and contemporary commentators often speak of the range of expression in common use. The profusion of dynamic indications as we understand them therefore has its origin in the desire of composers to break the rules, and the need to have musicians apply expression in ways and places they would normally avoid. One may assume, then, that as musicians grew more and more used to being told what to do it became necessary even to indicate hitherto normal practice.

During the modern Early Music revival some zealous pioneers, reading contemporary treatises and seeking to purge pre-Romantic music of Romantic-style expression, seem to have misinterpreted normal seventeenth- and eighteenth-century rules of expression as being curious and odd, whereas many of these were simply advice about performing in good taste, and hence forever pertinent. Consequently certain bizarre exaggerations became an accepted part of Baroque expression. These are to be eschewed, not perpetuated! Nor are mannerisms that can be traced to the traditional modern-Romantic style valid in Baroque music: these, therefore, should also be avoided, except in deliberate violation of good taste.

My purpose in this section of the book, then, is to set down as carefully and clearly as possible a basic, conventional approach to interpretation as it might have been understood by musicians in the seventeenth and eighteenth centuries: what you choose to do interpretatively, of course, comes under the heading of artistic prerogative, for art often lies in learning the rules and then selectively breaking them. First, however, one must know the rules.

Affect and Rhetoric

Two of the most important considerations in interpreting Baroque music are the emotional message, or *affect,* and *rhetoric,* the art of oration. Rhetoric, the art of communication, was one of the subjects in the *trivium*—the basic curriculum in medieval universities—and continued to be a component of a complete education until the nineteenth century. An essential tool of actors and orators, it was therefore also used by musicians in conveying their emotional message effectively. The songs of the *troubadours* and *trouvères* dealt mainly with courtly love, and their purpose was not only to entertain but, according to one contemporary music theorist,[1] to move the royal or noble listener to act with fortitude and magnanimity.

Commentaries on musical performance in the seventeenth and eighteenth centuries are replete with references to the expressive power of music and descriptions of its effect on various performers. Philosophers such as René Descartes (1596–1650) were fascinated by the power of music to stir emotions in the listener, and strove to understand the physiological cause. Johann Mattheson (1681–1764), a prominent German music theorist and composer, proposed an exhaustive "doctrine of the affections"[2] in which the various means of communicating emotions through music were examined in detail.

Music was likened to speech, and instruments to the human voice. Geminiani contributed this:

> *Men of purblind Understandings, and half Ideas may perhaps ask, is it possible to give Meaning and Expression to Wood and Wire; or to bestow upon them the Power of raising and soothing the Passions of rational Beings? But whenever I hear such a question put. . . . I shall make no difficulty to answer in the Affirmative, and without searching over-deeply into the Cause, shall think it sufficient to appeal to the Effect.*[3]

Canadian musicologist Mary Cyr sums up the aesthetic concept in these words: "The Baroque concept of affect was deeply rooted in the belief in the soul exerting control over the body and filling it with passions that are strongly expressed."[4]

Whereas it is relatively simple (and most important) to deduce the appropriate affect in the accompaniment of a vocal piece from its text, when interpreting Baroque and Classical instrumental music one must decipher clues hidden in the notes themselves, for composers of that period rarely provided specific verbal or symbolic instructions other than "tempo" indications as to the mood or moods to be conveyed.

When coaching students I often ask: "What is your affect?" for this, once the notes are familiar, is the most important next step in learning any piece. In this section of the book, then, I shall discuss the various stylistic and affective elements of a satisfactory interpretation.

The Role of Analysis

The organization of music has parallels in literature: just as books have chapters, paragraphs, sentences, and clauses, musical compositions have movements, sections, subsections, phrases, and gestures. A crucial and basic part of musical interpretation, then, is the identification of the divisions and subdivisions of a composition. Some, such as movements, or metrically or tonally contrasting sections, are obvious, but the smaller the subdivision, the harder it can be to recognize and to know where it starts and finishes.

The two elements that determine the organization of a musical composition are melody and harmony, and the learning process must involve careful analysis of both. Indeed, an invaluable component of this process—and a timesaving device—is studying the music without the instrument. Physical note-learning requires a degree of technical discipline that can distract from the analytical, and it is best to separate the two, especially when studying a polyphonic or harmonically complex work.

Treble players have a natural tendency to focus on the melodic line, especially if it is technically challenging. From the compositional viewpoint, however, the bass-line is more important, and to arrive at a convincing interpretation one must pay constant attention to it, for the tension between melody and bass and the harmonization linking the two are critical factors in determining affect and dynamic shaping.

The Importance of the Bass-Line

In order to create the most satisfactory linear effect in the dynamics of a phrase it is first essential to understand its harmonic, melodic, and logical structure. In Baroque music one must always be aware of the bass-line. Whereas in accompanied music this is already composed and audible, in music for solo instrument without figured bass one needs to identify the bass notes, some of which are written but others only inferred. For example, here is some music by Telemann in which the bass notes are obvious:

Once the bass-line is identified, the next step is to discern the harmonic structure, hearing each chord and being aware of its duration. Sometimes a harmony will change while the bass note remains constant, as in a simple 6/4–5/3 progression:

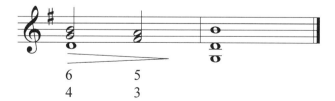

In this case, with the stronger 6/4 resolving on the weaker 5/3, a *diminuendo* is appropriate.

A slight variation of this harmonic progression, however, can alter the expression noticeably:

An important principle of interpretation to bear in mind, then, is that a dissonance will always be stronger than the consonance on which it resolves.

Once the harmonic framework of a passage is understood the nature of the melodic line must be considered, and the direction of the melody in relation to that of the bass is a critical factor. There are three possibilities: parallel motion, diverging, and converging. Take the same example from the Telemann B-flat Fantasie: here the lines diverge for three measures and then, in the fourth, converge to conclude the phrase unit. The implicit dynamic shape is *crescendo* for three bars with a slight *diminuendo* in the fourth, although Telemann, in ending the phrase unit with an unresolved dominant seventh—the rhetorical device of the Question—leaves it hanging:

In his E-flat Fantasie the bass and melodic lines are in parallel downward motion, and should, with the exception of the second half of measure two where the strong dominant ninth occurs, be played with a gradual *diminuendo*, reflecting the direction of the tessitura. The bass-line is obvious for the first three measures, and then moves up to F on the fourth. (The implicit bass note at the beginning of the third measure is B-flat, moving to E-flat on the third quarter-note.)

Another excerpt from Telemann's B-flat Fantasie demonstrates the effect of converging lines: here the bass notes rise from B-flat to G while the treble falls from B-flat to G, approaching from the lower *appoggiatura*, F-sharp, and the overall dynamic shape is *diminuendo*.

At times one encounters a florid passage in which the bass notes are disguised or only inferred, and here it is essential to identify them in order to understand clearly the harmonic structure of the music. One such instance occurs in the first section of Bach's Ciaccona:

Note the short-long, long-short rhythmic variety of the bass, which is characteristic of the *chaconne*. As for its dynamic structure, the basic shape conforms to its four-measure falling direction, while the floridity of the improvisatory-style writing demands great flexibility and range of nuance within that structure.

Always listen to the bass-line!

It is impossible to overemphasize this point. The same melody with a different bass, even unharmonized, will be played quite differently, for intervallic relationships by themselves imply certain harmonies. The bass-line not only dictates the harmonic structure of the movement but can also suggest *rubato* and influence the choice of tempo. Frequently it will imitate or anticipate the melodic line, and except for passages in which its role is static, when the melodic voice has a cadenza or extended *melismata* over a pedal tone, be a full partner.

In the ideal sonata relationship, an experienced and sensitive continuo player will allow the melody instrumentalist rhythmic freedom and flexibility while supporting the melodic line with an appropriately realized figured bass and, where needed, interesting, unobtrusively improvised *contreparties*. The "soloist," for his or her part, will be ever conscious of the continuist's contributions and, in turn, be released and inspired to take risks, to improvise as appropriate, and to shape the melodic line with spontaneous expression.

There *is* no such thing as "unaccompanied" music! In a movement of solo Bach—or a Telemann *Fantasie,* or the Biber *Passacaglia,* or any such piece—the bass-line is built into the music, and for an informed interpretation it is imperative that the player be keenly aware of its presence and function. An essential part, then, of the study of these works is analysis. One must identify the bass-notes, real or implied, and determine the harmonies above them in order to comprehend fully the dynamic shape and phrasing of the piece.

At times the note will only be there by implication, as in this example from Bach's G-minor *Adagio:*

In some modern editions, the 16th-note flag of the A on the downbeat of the second measure in the autograph has been misinterpreted, and a D added beneath the 6th thereby creating a D-major triad, a weak consonance. The correct bass-note, however, is C, which provides a strong foundation and creates an intense dissonance:

The implicit bass-note, C, causes great dissonant tension—a ninth with the D in the melody. Since the C will be inaudible to the listener, it is up to the player to react to the imagined (and yet real) dissonance and convey the dramatic effect. In light of this, appropriate nuances for this passage might be:

It is important also to understand that *adagio* rhetorical gestures such as this often require silence in order to be most effective. Here, after such a climactic gesture, for the temporarily unresolved dissonance to have the greatest impact one needs to pause briefly before continuing. Bach and his contemporaries were not about to clutter their music with such indications—for them it would have been unnecessary and, worse still, insulting to the performer. Today's interpreters, however, must learn to perceive that which was obvious to their eighteenth century predecessors.

The Tyranny of the Bar Line

Somehow, in the early days of the Early Music movement, most probably as a result of reading more into a musical principle than was ever intended, the habit of accenting the first note of each measure became common. One source of this is the set of rules recorded by Georg Muffat (1653–1704) in the preface to his *Florilegium Secundum,* published in 1695, which laid out in strict, methodical manner the performance practices of *Les 24 violons du Roi,* the orchestra that accompanied Jean-Baptiste Lully's *Comédie-ballets.* According to Muffat, the one inviolable principle of their style of bowing was the use of a down-bow on the downbeat of each measure. Whereas the obvious purpose of this was to make the rhythm absolutely clear to the dancers, when carelessly applied in other contexts it makes no sense and can have the result of causing the music to sound "beaty" and counted, interrupting the natural flow and drawing attention away from what is most important. There was, however, a contemporary backlash against what Geminiani referred to as "that wretched rule of the down-bow," and, in the Italian style, musicians chose their bowings more for convenience than because of any particular rule of accentuation. In Geminiani's treatise he gave bowing exercises to develop facility, some of which are deliberately obtuse and awkward almost to the point of impracticability, but evidently to ensure that his pupils could execute any phrase tastefully regardless of bow direction.

The concept of stress and release in music is certainly an important one, as is the accentuation of particular notes for expressive effect, but—as with any expressive device—the degree and manner of its implementation must always be governed by taste and context. In dance music, indeed, the character of each dance and its rhythmic structure is defined by the accentuation of certain notes and the release of others. A lively, energetic dance such as a *bourrée* requires greater contrast of strong and weak notes than does a more sorrowful or philosophical one like a *sarabande.* In a *menuet* measure the second and third quarter-notes must be "let go" (played lightly) and the third unaccented in order for the dance to have its characteristic lilt, and the music must be grouped in two-measure units.

Frequently in Baroque music, because of an irregularity in the number of bars in a phrase or the hierarchy of harmonies, the "downbeat" will occur on another subdivision of the measure, and for this reason it is important to understand both the harmonic structure of the music and the function of the metrical accent. A common error is to overlook the fact that a downbeat is now weaker and to accent it inappropriately. The following excerpt from Telemann's *Concerto in A Minor for Recorder and Viola da Gamba* demonstrates the way in which harmonic progression and melodic contour govern the placement of strong and weak accents. Notice the ambiguity and fluctuation of nuance as suggested by the dynamics and stress marks I have supplied, whereby stronger harmonies fall on the unstressed subdivision of the bar, a frequent occurrence in Baroque music:

The Significance of Metre

To underscore the significance of metre, I teach my students that "all music is in one." This concept has its origins in the medieval tradition of *tactus,* the practice of giving one downbeat and one upbeat per measure, that is, one strong and one weak beat. Applied to later music, in which regular bar lines are the norm, it helps to determine the frequency and position of stresses. In a simple quadruple passage such as the following from Bach's D-minor *Allemande:*

or a compound quadruple passage such as the opening of the D-minor *Giga:*

the stress falls on the downbeat and the un-stress on the third.

Consider, then, what would happen if the same passages were written in $\frac{2}{4}$ or $\frac{6}{8}$ instead. Here, again, the stress would be on each downbeat, but how would the music be changed? One difference would be in the tempo of the piece: if the *tactus* concept were applied, the eighth-notes in these examples would move more slowly. To understand this, imagine that eighth-notes in $\frac{2}{4}$ have the same function as quarter-notes in $\frac{4}{4}$—that they constitute the simple subdivision of the measure. Visualize a metronome and imagine that quarter-notes in $\frac{4}{4}$ are sped up until they can go no faster, at which point they become the eighth-notes in a $\frac{2}{4}$. Apply the *tactus* rule, and the third eighth-note is now unstressed.

Take, for example, the opening passage of Bach's A-minor *Fuga:*

Strictly speaking, however, this fugal theme is a type of *alla breve,* in which the odd-numbered bars are pickups to the even-numbered. The metrical sign ¢, known as *alla breve,* originally indicated that strong beats were to occur on every other measure.[5] Hence, in a typical passage, such as the theme of his C-major *Fuga,* whose basic unit is the half-note, the quarter-notes move quite rapidly:

In this fugue subject the downbeats occur on bars 1 and 3, the upbeats on bars 2 and 4.

The pairing of measures according to the dictates of metre or harmonic structure is a common device in much Baroque and Classical music. When this happens, the second measure is often the "weaker" of the two, harmonically or melodically, and should therefore normally be relatively unstressed. Here is another way of indicating *alla breve,* as used by Bach in his G-minor *Presto* and other movements:

A commonly used formula for a phrase unit in eighteenth-century music is the *Sentence*—what I refer to colloquially as the "one-one-two" or "short-short-long." The opening of Bach's D-minor *Sarabanda* contains an example:

This classic method of organization results in a stress occurring on each of the first three bars of a four-bar unit and none on the fourth.

In all the preceding discussion and description of the various types of organization, the word "stress" has occurred quite frequently. It is important to understand, however, that this is simply a way of defining the function of a note, an indication that the principal notes of gestures and phrases should be clear but not necessarily emphatic. Beware of over-accentuation, which is one of the exaggerations that give Early Music a bad name!

Shaping Notes and Gestures

The shaping of individual notes and gestures is one of the most useful and important expressive devices in Baroque performance practice. Geminiani categorizes most bow strokes as good, bad, or special (*particolare*), and the only stroke that is described as good at any tempo is one for which he uses his crescendo[6] symbol, although Leopold Mozart, in his *Versuch einer gründlichen Violinschule*, advises: "*Every note, even the strongest attack, has a small, even barely audible, softness at the beginning of the stroke; for it would otherwise be no note but only an unpleasant and unintelligible noise. This same softness must be heard also at the end of each stroke.*"[7] The degree of swell or decay of a stroke should be determined by the affective context. A note of any duration can be expressive of a variety of tempi and moods depending on its shape. For instance, a note one-second long played with a strong attack and a swift decay gives the impression of *allegro,* whereas a note of the same duration played with a gentle swell may be expressive of a tender, more pensive mood and a slower tempo.

One error in right-hand technique is so common among violin students that I have come to refer to it as the "violin-thing." This is the habit of drawing a down-bow so rapidly that the sound decays to inaudibility, whereupon the player has to insert a rest into the musical line while waiting for the next note to occur, or else, having overlooked the need for a swell toward the end of the note, makes a weak, strangled sound instead of an expressive one. Here, again, context is everything, and one must always take the harmonic structure and melodic line into account in determining the character of each note or gesture.

Another fault to avoid is a habit so prevalent among cellists that I refer to it as the "cello-thing." This is what occurs, typically on the note preceding the bar line: a cellist leans forward, makes a *crescendo,* and elides with the note on the downbeat. Certainly this is desirable in some instances, as with a chromatic upbeat, but even then it is best, in Baroque and Classical music, to articulate almost imperceptibly so as to give the new note a clear start. Remember that when a composer wants absolute *legato,* there will be a slur, but by the end of the slur there will always be a certain degree of *diminuendo.*

A suspension should usually be sustained or swelled, and the first note after the suspension always played more softly, without accent. Bow speed and the pressure of the first finger are crucial factors, as is the use of the fourth finger to control the weight of the bow. An exception may be made when the note occurs at the end of a section and is followed by an anacrusis. Consider the following excerpt from Bach's G-minor *Adagio:*

It is appropriate, since the tied octave D marks the end of a long section, to allow it to taper rather than anticipating the *crescendo* that occurs naturally on the following ornamental flurry leading to the sharp 6/4 and creates a much more dramatic gesture.

The suspended E-flat, however, requires an intense *crescendo* to join the F-sharp, and even though the succeeding notes should be "let go" so as not to upstage it, the G-minor resolution, with its Lombardic *appoggiatura,* can be even stronger.

The "banana-shaped note" is another common form of exaggeration. This is the nickname given to a note played with an excessive *messa di voce.* The *messa di voce* is a vocal ornament described in early-seventeenth-century treatises such as *Le nuove musiche,*[8] whereby a long note is swelled; but, as with any ornament, too frequent or exaggerated use detracts from its effectiveness, and the notes so treated stand out from the musical texture in an unpleasant way. This is especially true of notes of longer value but short duration, such as half-notes or dotted quarters.

In principle, most notes in any passage should be shaped in some way and to some degree, according to context and affect. The use of organ-like droning is usually reserved for pedal accompaniment—it is rarely necessary to play straight, uninflected tones other than for such a purpose. Apart from dramatic effects such as the *esclamazione*—another vocal ornament, in which the note is relatively strongly attacked, with an immediate drop in dynamic followed by a swell—the subtle warming of a note by a slight increase in bow speed or pressure is useful for creating interesting expression, and therefore most desirable.

Here is an important concept: **Think in terms of "sounds," not notes.**

A sound can consist of one note or many, slurred or unslurred, A group of notes under a slur should be thought of as a single sound whose degree of complexity is directly proportional to the number of notes contained in it. Obviously the more notes there are under a slur, the more one can shape them.

Take the following passage from Bach's D-minor *Allemanda,* for example:

The dynamics I have suggested correspond to the contours of the melody, to the tessitura and to the number of notes under each slur. Leopold Mozart said that notes under a slur are to be played with a *diminuendo,* but in the above passage this can only be true of the four-note slurs; otherwise the notes under the longer slurs would be quite inexpressive. I prefer to say that when notes are slurred a *diminuendo* will occur *sooner or later.* Once again, context is everything.

To return to the concept of sounds: the notes in the above example do not themselves constitute a melodic line—those in the first bar and a half are simply an improvisation on the dominant seventh on E, escalating dynamically for purely violinistic reasons: without forcing, one cannot play sixteen notes in a bow as loudly as one can play eight.[9] Each of these slurred groups constitutes one sound. The second of these is louder, resulting in an escalation of tension and leading to the first truly melodic notes, the first of each of the four-note groups in the descending sequence. The natural shape of each of these sounds is a tapering, while the entire sequence falls away dynamically.

The absence of slurs need not mean that notes are to be played evenly, and, especially in contrapuntal music, groups of notes should often be treated as though they were individual sounds. Here is an excerpt from the *Double* of Bach's B-minor *Corrente* in which each of nine groups of separately bowed notes can best be considered in that way:

Each one is a harmonic entity—in the first bar a series of three $^6_3$ triads, then the chord of the seventh on C-sharp resolving to a $^6_5$, and so on. The falling sequences dictate the use of *diminuendi,* and within the overall *diminuendo* each four-note group needs to have its own:

When played in this way, the result is a lightness of execution that best expresses the excitement of the affect while at the same time making the hierarchy of the contrapuntal lines easily perceptible.

Beware of the Beam!

At some point in the seventeenth century the use of beams to group and organize notes became standard, but in much of seventeenth-century music the notes have separate stems, a notational practice that carries over to the present day in vocal music (other than melismatic passages). An extreme example in the violin literature is to be found in the original printing of the sonatas of Carlo Farina (Dresden, 1628), in which there are neither beams nor bar lines. Needless to say, this may cause some difficulty when first reading these pieces, accustomed as we are to organizational clarity, but the more primitive notation has the effect of liberating us from the latter's mathematical stiffness. When notes are beamed in threes, fours, and sixes, the grouping does not necessarily reflect the harmonic and melodic organization of the music. Whereas music may be easier to count when notes are grouped under beams, the phrase or gesture can and often does end during a beamed group, as in Bach's D-minor *Giga:*

The commas here indicate points at which the primary rhythmic motif recurs, where one tapers the slur and plays the eighth-note as a pickup. At times composers clearly indicate such phrase organization by separating one note from the rest of a beamed group, but mostly it must be determined from other clues, such as context and harmony. In the above example, clarification of the sequential nature of the passage requires inflection, which, however, if notated, could result in over-phrasing.

The downbeat of the third measure of this passage is often played too weakly, as though cadential, and the second eighth-note stressed instead of being perceived (correctly) as part of the first inversion of the B-flat major chord that is the initial element of a brief descending sequence:

The Trouble with Notation

It is important to understand that our system of notation, based as it is on mathematical organization—twos and threes—is limited and imperfect. What any composer writes can generally only be an approximation of what he imagines. In some contexts, such as dances, of course, the notes will need to be a precise rendering of what he hears; but more frequently, especially in much Baroque music, one must "read between the lines" and apply certain conventions when performing that result in the music being less precisely rhythmic and more flexible. This is a practice loosely referred to as "rhythmic alteration." For example, most of us are familiar with the Viennese waltz, and the remarkable sense of motion imparted by the slight irregularity of the accompanying quarter-notes, which are quite regularly notated.

Another familiar instance today occurs in jazz in the way eighth-notes are "swung." This has a counterpart in the French Baroque convention known as *notes inégales,* whereby a passage in $\frac{3}{4}$ or $\frac{4}{4}$, written in even eighth-notes, will be played in such a way that the odd-numbered notes are slightly longer and heavier than the even-numbered, creating a lightly flowing motion. Most significant, however, is that it is not possible to notate this effect: it can only be described. More extreme versions of this effect, such as long-short triplets, or dotted eighth- and sixteenth-notes, which *are* notated, are reserved for compositions such as *gigues* and marches, which derive their energy from consistently precise rhythms.

As a consequence of the un-notatability of *notes inégales,* the instructions in most primary source material,[10] apart from the vague description given above, have to do with when not to use them! Here is the list:

When the composer has written dots over the notes

When the composer specifically asks for *notes égales*

In passages of leaping, energetic notes

Where three or more notes are slurred

When a passage is too fast (and would sound hectic as a result)

On notes shorter than the first subdivision of the metre

On triplets or in triple or compound duple metres

On repeated notes

Apart from passages governed by these restrictions, then, it is normal in French or French-style music of the Baroque to play in this gently lilting style. One must be careful, however, not to do so in a predictable, regular way but to vary, subtly, the degree of *inegalité*. In a passage such as the following, for instance,

the eighth-notes could start in a quasi-triplet rhythm, gradually smoothing out to a more or less equal relationship by the end of the bar. The last two notes might even be gently *lombardic*, that is, short-long. Typical among movements that require this treatment are *menuets, courantes françaises* and *sarabandes*.

Rhythmic alteration of another sort is applied to dotted notes in a process known as "over-dotting."[11] The following figures can be interpreted in various ways depending on affect and context:

As a point of departure, consider that the longer of the two notes is the more important, which in the language of Baroque music means that the shorter one will be played more lightly. But as for the relative length of the notes, the range may extend from extreme over-dotting to quasi-triplet, depending on the context in which the figure occurs. Indeed, it is possible, when both figures appear in the same passage, for the eighth-note to have the same value as the sixteenth. By way of illustration, in the following excerpt from Bach's *Ciaccona*, in order to give the dance its characteristic lilt the eighth-notes of the movement's opening bars should already be as short and light as the sixteenths in the next section:

Here is another way of writing (and reading) the first four measures:

In this way a smooth transition is also made to the second eight-bar section. Historical justification for this interpretation of the rhythm may be found in Leopold Mozart's treatise, when, referring to the dotted rhythm, he said, "We play it this way (with the longer note sustained), so why not write it thus?" and illustrated his point using double dots, a type of notation not current at the time.

Long-short triplet notation, which we now take for granted, was not in common use until well into the nineteenth century. Here, in Bach's B-minor *Corrente*, is a passage in which the dotted rhythm, because of the context, can be taken to mean lilting triplets:

The dotted figures should still have a dancelike character, the notes clearly articulated, but playing them literally, as dotted eighths and sixteenths, would draw attention to the pattern instead of having them blend into the affective scenery.

When playing Classical music, one often encounters a passage in which a dotted note is preceded by an *appoggiatura* and followed by a note one-third its value. Note the way in which the dotted rhythm is preserved in this example cited by Leopold Mozart, for which he gives the following instructions:

With dotted notes the appoggiatura is held the same length of time as the value of the note. In place of the dot, however, the written note is taken first, and in such fashion as if a dot stood after it. Then the bow is lifted and the last note played so late that, by means of a rapid change of stroke, the note following it is heard immediately after.[12]

One final point: Baroque composers were less concerned with what is possible on the instrument than with the logic of voice-leading, and so one finds many notes that cannot be played as they look on paper. A typical example is the final chord of the Adagio of Bach's G-minor *Solo Sonata*, which is a whole-note tetrachord.[13] Another example from Bach's A-minor *Fuga:*

Without going into more detail, one should not slur the eighth-notes in such passages simply because of the quarter-notes above them. In order to give the impression that the quarter-notes are *legato*, it is only necessary to sustain the quarters for the full value of an eighth while releasing and articulating the eighths and sixteenths.

Similarly, with moving, separate notes under a suspension, as in the following example from Bach's C-major *Fuga,* it is a mistake to play them slurred, which introduces a dense texture foreign to the prevailing fugal clarity:

The quarter-notes can easily be articulated while sustaining the tied half-notes—starting down-bow, the entire passage may be played "as it comes" to very good effect.

The Reality of *Rubato*

A popular misconception among modern musicians is that *tempo rubato* should only be associated with the Romantic era, in music of composers such as Chopin and Liszt, and that Baroque music is to be performed strictly. As early as the beginning of the seventeenth century, however, composers and theorists were writing about rhythmic flexibility. For information on this topic we may draw upon the writings of Girolamo Frescobaldi, in the advice given to the reader in prefaces to his books of toccatas, and Giulio Caccini in his preface to *Le Nuove Musiche*. In Caccini's work he advocated the use of *sprezzatura*, a nonchalant approach, in the interpretation of monody. Frescobaldi, in the prefaces to his volumes of keyboard toccatas, exhorted the performer to allow the music to breathe, to move ahead, to linger, and so forth, in ways appropriate to the character or affect of particular passages.[14] None of this was indicated by expression marks such as those with which we are familiar but were to be inferred from the music itself. Obviously context is everything, and at times precise, regular rhythm is called for, especially in dancelike sections or movements, or in *ostinato* passages; but to apply this kind of strictness to lyrical pieces or, especially, *adagios* only makes the music rigid and unnatural, which defeats the composer's intention.

Essentially the function of *rubato* is to make music sound as natural and spontaneous as possible. That few expressive directions are given in Baroque and early Classical music permits the performer to approach it in a fresh and quasi-improvisatory way each time a piece is played, which is ideal. This is particularly true in an *Adagio,* where, because of the leisurely pace of the movement, one has time to react to particular harmonies and to use one's bow eloquently to shape the melodic line. One may allow oneself to experience the gravitational pull toward a dissonance and, having arrived, linger to enjoy the sensation before moving on. One finds a wonderful example in Bach's D-minor *Sarabanda:*

In such a place one should be careful to draw attention neither to the bar-line nor to the individual beamed groups but to create a gesture that starts somewhat slowly after the upbeat, flowing forward unimpeded to the briefly held A—which should be played as though reaching upward—and then falls gracefully toward the cadence.

The subtlest type of *rubato* is the "agogic accent." This is a slight lengthening of a note, a method used by keyboard players—organists and harpsichordists—to create emphasis. It may be gently used to good effect in passages such as this in Bach's G-minor *Fuga:*

Another method of accentuation employed by singers in seventeenth-century Italy was to delay a note slightly. A *diminuendo* and the slightest placement of the D-minor chord serve to emphasize this dramatic moment in Bach's A-minor *Grave:*

CHAPTER NINE

Dynamics and Nuance

Until the second half of the eighteenth century expression marks of any kind were relatively rare. Dynamics were limited mainly to the indication of echoes or the use in cantatas and concertos to alert the accompanying instruments that the solo voice was entering or leaving the texture. In mid-century, in the spirit of *Sturm und Drang,* composers began experimenting with the addition of unusual and dramatic effects, asking performers to make dynamic contrasts in places and ways that, because of their training, would be unexpected. This was the genesis of dynamic indications as we understand them.

In the Baroque era, though, most expressive clues were contained in the music, and whereas to the untrained modern eye there would seem to be no dynamics, the performer of the day could clearly perceive the composer's intention. Here are some of the keys to understanding the dynamic structure of music composed prior to the time when expression began to be prescribed:

    a. Harmony: Knowledge of the various types of consonances and dissonances and of the relationship of chords to one another.

    b. Melody: Awareness of its contours and the significance of *tessitura*—the range of a voice and the changing distance between the bass and the melodic line.

    c. Figures of musical speech: Recognition of the various rhetorical devices commonly used by composers, and their function.

Harmony

Harmony as we understand it was not codified until well into the eighteenth century—in 1722—when Jean-Philippe Rameau published his *Traité de l'harmonie.* Early Baroque music was still based on the modal system, and only in the late seventeenth century were composers such as Arcangelo Corelli and his teacher Maurizio Cazzati, *maestro di capellla* of San Petronio in Bologna, experimenting with the tonal system, which was later to become standard. Nowadays, in the twenty-first century, we have heard everything imaginable in the way of harmony (and dissonance), but if we are to appreciate fully its significance in earlier music, we must endeavor to hear the music through the ears of musicians of the time.

We tend to flatter ourselves that whatever existed prior to our own time was, by definition, inferior—instruments, performance standards, the degree of sophistication, and so on. What happened, however, was an evolutionary streamlining process that eliminated many of the features once considered a normal part of music-making. These included harpsichords with split keys capable of playing the enharmonic scale; a variety of temperaments that gave each key its own unique character; the art of ornamentation; and families of instruments that would blend and balance effortlessly not only with one another but also with members of other families.

The alternation of dissonance and consonance is an essential component of tonal musical language, and composers in the Baroque era were responsible for dramatic developments in the use of this device. Whereas at first, with mean-tone temperaments, only a limited number of keys were available, some composers exploited the situation and wrote passages replete with the most extreme dissonances.[1] At the height of the Baroque era a temperament was in use by which, in the cycle of 5ths, each major third became slightly wider, thereby creating an increasingly pungent V-I cadential sequence. According to Mark Linley,[2] the Preludes and Fugues in Bach's *Well-Tempered Clavier*, when played using this tuning system, sound best in the key in which they were written and cannot effectively be transposed. It is almost certain that Bach was not using equal temperament.

There are those who argue that equal temperament is a good thing: after all, they say, it solves the problem of the comma most efficiently, and you don't really notice that no interval other than the octave is in tune, so slightly are they out of tune. I would counter that equal temperament means the absence of all temperament, for the palpable contrasts in tension that characterize dominant-tonic relationships in earlier tuning systems are eliminated, as are the exquisitely more dissonant harmonies. (Of course, a pianist can choose to compensate for this by creating dynamic nuances that were unavailable to harpsichordists.)

How, then, can harmonies influence the dynamic shape of a piece?

If one considers the dominant-tonic progression, for example, where the tension of the dominant chord is relieved by the consonant resolution of the cadence, it is most natural to play the dominant more strongly than the tonic. A V-I cadence, therefore, has an implicit *diminuendo*.

The opposite is true with a I-V cadence, such as is frequently found at the double-bar in an AABB movement, before the repeat of the first section: here the appropriate dynamic progression is weak-strong, or *crescendo*, which, in turn, prepares the way for the return to the tonic when one makes the repeat. However, in the second section of a binary movement, starting on the dominant, the naturally stronger dynamic has been prepared, and when the second section is repeated, the dynamic progression from the concluding tonic back to the double-bar is, once again, weak-strong. One option, a rhetorical device recommended in eighteenth-century sources, is to play the repeat even more strongly, since one function of repetition is to reinforce ideas already presented, and this is particularly effective in the case of the repeat of the second part of a movement.

A critical ingredient in the effective interpretation of Baroque music is awareness of the bass-line and of the harmonic tension between melody and bass. Even where the composer has not provided figures to indicate the chords, there are conventional progressions that an experienced accompanist will read into the notes. One must therefore be ever sensitive to fluctuations of consonance and dissonance, and react to them with varied bow speed and pressure, playing dissonances, such as those created by *appoggiature,* more strongly than the consonances that precede and follow them, or, when playing a suspension, swelling toward the dissonance at the end. Here I would point out once again that there is no such thing as "unaccompanied" Baroque music, for the bass-line is built into the melodic texture and dictates nuances even when it can only be inferred.

Melody

In Baroque music a melody may be *cantabile* and thus readily recognizable as such, but it may also be concealed in a florid texture, in which case one must identify the actual melodic notes and, in a sense, extract them from that texture. In either case certain conventions apply that affect the shape of the gestures and phrases.

The direction of a melodic line has an important dynamic function: basically, if a melodic line—as defined by the actual melodic notes, not the ornamental figures in which they are concealed—rises, it is normal to make a *crescendo,* and when it falls, a *diminuendo.* By way of illustration, let's look at this theme in Vivaldi's *Winter:*

If we extract the basic melodic notes and base our interpretation of the dynamics on those, the shape is as follows:

The ornamental figures, falling or rising, will be played with a subtle *diminuendo,* and the shaping of the phrase might therefore be

Notice that the last note of each measure other than 4 and 8 will be softer than the start of the next. In this way the basic melodic notes stand subtly out from the texture. The ninth measure, because it's a dominant chord, will be held up dynamically but still soft enough to allow for a sequential *crescendo* in the following four bars. In measure 8 there should be a *crescendo* in the bass: upward chromatic alteration in Baroque music always signifies an increase in tension—the opposite, though a beautiful effect, belongs to a later age.

Figures of Musical Speech

REPETITION

A device all too commonly used in modern performances and performing editions of Baroque and Classical music (one that generally speaks of a lack of imagination on the part of the editor or performer) is the echo. This is a natural phenomenon, and when a composer in the period prior to the end of the eighteenth century, when dynamic indications had become a normal feature, wanted that effect, it would be written into the music. Indeed, this is generally the only dynamic indication to be provided by early composers. In its absence, the other possible interpretation of the repetition of a phrase or gesture that may be used to good effect is the opposite—*più forte*—for its purpose can be the reinforcement of an idea, or emphasis.

When a note is repeated several times a *crescendo* is often effective unless the notes are slurred; the implication of the slur, with or without *staccato* dots, is a *diminuendo*, especially when the harmony is a resolving dissonance:

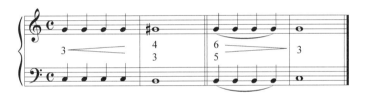

SEQUENCES

Another frequently used musical effect is the sequence, whereby a pattern is repeated several times, in rising or falling transposition. In a descending sequence it is normal to make a *diminuendo*, and conversely, when rising, a *crescendo*, as in this passage from Bach's D-minor *Allemande*:

This is analogous to the rhetorical device often used by politicians and evangelical preachers, whereby a phrase is repeated several times, changing one word at each repetition.

TESSITURA

An important consideration in deciding on an appropriate dynamic level is the *tessitura* of the bass-line. In general, one may assume that the higher the bass-line and the closer it is to the melody, the softer the dynamic. Hence, this section of Bach's

C-major *Fuga,* where the alto becomes the lowest voice, should be played much more delicately than the preceding passage:

When two lines diverge, there will be a *crescendo:*

Conversely, when they converge, there will be a *diminuendo.* Note, however, that where the bass-line drops an octave in this example, the dynamic level will increase accordingly:

(The dynamics indicated in both examples are my own suggestion—none appear in the original music, composed by Gaetano Pugnani.)

Here is a classic example of diverging lines in a sonata by Corelli:

Note that the bass-line starts only a third below the melody, indicating a dynamic low point, but then the rapid divergence signals a dramatic *crescendo* to the climax of the phrase.

Similarly, in this variation in Corelli's *La Follia,* as two lines diverge one should make a *crescendo,* and as they converge, a *diminuendo.*[3]

The direction of the musical line, then, can often be an indication of the dynamic contour of the music. All other things being equal, when a melody is rising, it is natural for the dynamic level to grow with it, and when it falls, to decrease. This is, of course, simplistic, for a number of factors need to be taken into consideration when deciding on an interpretation; however, it is a useful point of departure.

I define "musical line" as a sequence of purely melodic notes, with the secondary, ornamental ones removed, as demonstrated above in the fragment of Vivaldi's *Winter.* The shorter, ornamental notes, even when moving upward, are to be treated with a slight *diminuendo,* for making a *crescendo* would be inelegant and heavy-handed.

The same is usually true in the case of arpeggiated chords, such as these in Bach's D-minor *Giga,* rising from a bass note on the beat. In this descending sequence, moving in half-bar units, the even-numbered beats are weaker than the odd, and the next beat is again stronger but within the overall framework of the *diminuendo.*

THE QUESTION

When a composer interrupts the flow of the music with a strong dissonance, causing the music to hang in the air momentarily before continuing, it is as if he has asked a question, and the continuation of the music is the answer. For instance, in Bach's G-minor *Adagio:*

In such a place it is appropriate to hesitate a moment before resuming.

THE EXCLAMATION

Here are some examples of exclamations in Bach. They can be complete gestures, such as this sudden expostulation:

or just single chords, such as the exultant ending of the C-major *Fuga:*

At times, with characteristic ambiguity, they may take the form of a particularly emphatic *question,* as in this moment in the E-major *Gavotte:*

Note that it is important to relax the sound before the accented note or chord in order to have the best effect. It is a mistake to make a *crescendo,* which undercuts the surprise element. Delaying the accent slightly can also heighten its effectiveness.

SILENCE

Silence is a powerful rhetorical device. I have referred frequently to the use of articulation to energize and clarify the texture of a musical line, for as stringed instrumentalists we are capable of playing until we drop without ever interrupting the continuity of our sound. Unlike singers and wind and brass players, we don't need to take occasional breaths unless the composer has built them into the music in the form of rests. Besides subtle articulation, however, we must also be keenly aware of the occasional need for silence for dramatic purposes and on the lookout for opportunities to make use of it. The passage quoted earlier from Bach's G-minor *Adagio* provides a vivid illustration:

CHAPTER TEN

Tempo

As early as the sixteenth century Galileo was experimenting with ways of keeping time in music, and before the invention of the metronome in 1815 other means were employed to calculate and indicate appropriate tempi. For the modern player, accustomed to being provided with a metronome mark—the number of "beats" per minute, or a "tempo mark" such as *allegro* or *adagio*—the absence of any such indication can at first be confusing and perplexing. The choice of a suitable tempo is influenced by a number of factors, some having to do with the form, some with the music's technical complexity or harmonic structure, and some with the period or the country in which the composer lived.

Metrical Symbols

One essential method of tempo indication is the use of metrical symbols to indicate the number of beats or impulses in a measure. This has its origin in the early method of beating time in choral music, giving the strong and weak beats or *tactus*. These symbols had an important function in the calculation of tempo: not only the basic tempo but also of proportional transitions within a piece.

Tempo *ordinario*, also known as "common time," is so called because the basic beat is approximately equal to that of the normal human pulse—roughly eighty beats per minute. In the absence of any qualification, then, this is a convenient way of understanding what tempo a composer had in mind when using the symbol "C."

Alla breve, so-called cut-time ¢, now indicates, especially to an orchestral musician, that the music will be beaten in two and therefore "twice as fast," or at least "faster." *Alla breve* is a concept whose meaning has changed over the centuries; it originally signified that the strong beat (*tactus*) was given on the odd-numbered measures and the weak beat (or "upbeat") on the even—hence one downbeat every two measures. Much Baroque music is organized in two-measure units, and the *alla breve* concept may be applied wherever this occurs: a strong measure followed by a weak measure, and hence a strong beat followed by a weaker beat. In Johann Sebastian Bach's Sonatas and Partitas for Violin Solo one finds a different version of this—the use of the short bar line to subdivide two-measure units, a clear indication of his intention:

By extrapolation, then, the concept may be applied not only to beats within a measure but even to subdivisions of beats—the second of two eighth-notes, for instance, being played more lightly.

Harmonic Motion

Simply put, the more complex the harmonic structure of a movement, the slower the tempo should be relative to other, similar movements. A piece in which there are frequent changes of chord requires a more measured pace than one in which the harmony only changes every measure or two. Instances of the latter may be found in Bach's cello suites: In the opening phrases of the G-major *Prelude* (¢) each chord lasts for a whole measure; in the E-flat prelude (¢) the chord change comes only on the third measure. Both give a clear indication of easily flowing motion, and yet one often hears the eighth-note arpeggios of the E-flat *Prelude* played so slowly as to give the impression that each individual note is part of a stately melody!

Technical Complexity

Needless to say, the more technically complicated a movement for either hand, the more steadily it should be played. Some passages require a rapid tempo, however, in order to be melodically or even contrapuntally comprehensible. Certain passages in Bach and Corelli, for instance, are what I call kaleidoscopic: they must be played rapidly enough for inner voices to emerge from the texture—below a certain pace the individual melodic notes are lost in an amorphous, "notey" mass. Here is a simple illustration from Corelli's *Sonata in C Major*, op. 5, no. 3:

When the passage is played rapidly enough, the notes that emerge from the texture are as follows:

Affective Words

As modern musicians we are used to thinking of basic, unqualified tempo indications as meaning faster or slower. Perhaps this was also true in the eighteenth century; after all, Geminiani did devote a whole page of his treatise to a description of the appropriate bowing styles in "*adagio* or *andante*" tempi, versus "*allegro* or *presto*." "*Allegro*," however, does not literally mean fast nor "*andante*" slow, and I find it useful to consider the literal meanings of these and other words when deciding on tempi. Here are some examples:

allegro: "cheerful, bright, lively"

adagio: "with care, gently"

andante: "going"

largo: "wide, broad"

presto: "quickly"

vivace: "lively"

Note also that *allegro* and *vivace* are almost synonymous linguistically. How, then, are we to determine that difference musically? I personally prefer to think of *allegro* as meaning cheerful and lighthearted, and *vivace* as lively and energetic. Here are a couple of examples from unaccompanied Bach to illustrate my conception. Note that Bach himself qualified the first selection:

Allegro

In practice, little difference will be evident in the perceived tempo of the eighth-notes in these two fugue subjects, but even a cursory glance indicates the difference in their character. The melodic line of the G-minor subject is relatively smooth and tranquil, whereas that of the A minor is leaping about energetically: this sort of passage I would label *vivace.* Perhaps Bach thought it necessary to caution the performer against playing the G-minor subject, a falling figure, with too relaxed an affect despite the *alla breve* metre, and used *allegro* to signal his intention. Certainly, given the choice of metre and the energy of the subject, there was no need to tell the performer about the character of the A-minor *Fuga!* Generally, then, I choose to believe that if an identical passage were to be marked first *allegro* and then *vivace,* the latter would be somewhat slower because of the greater energy needed to play it.

Tempo indications were already used by some composers at the beginning of the seventeenth century, and in the music of Dario Castello we are given an interesting insight into the etymology of the word *adagio:* there it appears as *ad asio,* which means simply "at ease." Possibly *adagio* is a Venetian corruption, but the original form sheds light on the true sense of the term. In my teaching I advise students when they encounter the word to think of it as encouraging them to take time to be expressive, to play with flexibility, to "stop and enjoy the scenery" or "smell the flowers," and not just to play slowly, but certainly to use *rubato* whenever it seems appropriate. (In colloquial Italian, by the way, *"Adagio, adagio!"* means "Take it easy!")

Cautionary and Qualifying Words

Occasionally one encounters tempo indications that seem strangely contradictory or paradoxical, such as *largo e staccato* or *andante largo*. The former, *largo e staccato*, usually means that the whole piece is to be played at a broad, leisurely pace with well-detached bow strokes, but it can also indicate an alternation in melodic style, or possibly even that the bass line is to be played *staccato* while the melodic line is lyrical. In the latter case, *largo* is a qualification that suggests taking a slightly steadier tempo than if it were not there, for, as noted above, *andante* does not mean "slow." What it does mean, however, is that the tempo should be continuous, with hardly any *rubato:* when associated with a "walking" eighth-note bass line, the latter should be played fairly *staccato* and with constant direction.

I am reminded of two Baroque composers who were in the habit of using cautionary words to head off potential problems: Vivaldi and Leclair. By this I mean such indications as *presto ma non troppo* or *allegro ma poco* at the beginning of what seems to be a fairly straightforward, uncomplicated movement. Such words should always be taken seriously, for the reasons can either be technical or purely musical: the music must have time to breathe, or else a fast movement can become a *moto perpetuo.*

"Allowing the music to breathe" is an important aspect of interpretation. I often cite as an analogy the German Railroad clock, whose second hand, when it arrives at 60, waits a full second for the minute hand to catch up before starting again. (Obviously each click of the second hand is less than one second in duration!) This represents what one must do in music in order to organize phrases into intelligible units. Correctly done, the time taken is imperceptible but essential. If this is overdone, it draws attention to itself and the music limps; if it's not done at all, the music sounds breathless and even tends to accelerate. It is a simple way of controlling the motion of a piece while at the same time acknowledging its harmonic and melodic structure.

Baroque Dance Movements

Whereas Baroque dance had long since gone out of fashion by the twentieth century, in the past fifty years a considerable amount of research has been done in an effort to reconstruct the various forms and to understand their style and tempo. Experts in this area have located and translated treatises on dance notation and have thus been able to revive theatrical and social dances of the seventeenth and eighteenth centuries. The importance of the role of dance in social and even political life in that era can hardly be overemphasized. Dancing masters were employed to teach new steps, and there was no excuse for being unfamiliar with them. In any court everyone—royalty, nobility, clerics, courtiers, and musicians alike—was expected to be technically secure in the various dances on a daily basis! To be unprepared for the evening ball and thus disgrace oneself could result in humiliation, ridicule, even ostracism.

Most of the dances one finds in suites and *partitas* are, obviously, abstract—not intended for dancing on the stage or at a ball. What one cannot overlook, however, in the process of interpreting Baroque dances, is that composers were intimately familiar with all of them, both as spectators and as dancers! Thanks to the efforts of scholars, it is possible today for people to become familiar with Baroque dance, if not to become experts, and for those genuinely interested in learning the dances there are frequent classes and workshops. Here are some of the more common dances in our repertoire:

Allemande/Allemanda: There are different styles of *Allemande*. In late-seventeenth-century German music, as found in Biber's sonatas, for example, the dance has a light, lively character; in French music it is elegant; in the late-Baroque era, sometimes lively, sometimes reflective and philosophical. The single-note upbeat, written sometimes as a sixteenth-note, sometimes as an eighth, should always be short, falling lightly over the bar line.

Bourrée: This is a fast, energetic, vigorous dance, and is to be played with clearly lifted bow strokes.

Chaconne: By the late Baroque this dance had become much slower than its original version. Similar to the *Sarabanda* in that the basic rhythmic motif is short-long, except that it has an upbeat, whereas the *Sarabanda* does not. In the *Ciaccona* by Bach, it is important to be aware of the harmonic structure, for the movement alternates between *Chaconne* and *Passacaglia*. The harmonic structure of the *Chaconne* is such that the first D-minor chord is an upbeat, whereas in the *Passacaglia* sections the D-minor chord is the downbeat of the four-bar unit.

Corrente: This Italian-style dance movement should be played *allegro,* with lively energy, but never hurried.

Courante: An extremely elegant French dance, one of whose characteristics is the random alternation between $\frac{3}{2}$. and $\frac{6}{4}$, this is always to be played at a moderate tempo.

Gavotte: It is important to ensure that the two-quarter-note upbeat with which this graceful dance begins is played lightly, because usually, in the dance itself, there is no step until the downbeat.

Gigue/Giga: A dance whose triplet figure gives it a sprightly character. The tempo and metre will vary according to the style of writing—the pulse will normally be faster if the movement is composed only in eighth-notes than if it is in sixteenths. However, it should be joyous in mood rather than hurried. When the triplet figure is in dotted rhythm, the dance is referred to as a *Gigue louré*.

Loure: The rhythmic motif that identifies this dance is the short-long pickup. The *Loure* is a theatrical dance; the male version is faster—energetic and athletic—and the female, elegant and pensive. Regardless of tempo, the signature upbeat motif should be played with lift, not lyrically, the eighth-note shorter and more energetic than the notated value suggests.

Menuet: The name of this dance comes from the French *menu,* which means "tiny," reflecting the kind of steps used by the dancers. It is always organized in two-measure gestures and played at roughly quarter = 160, the third quarter-note of the bar never accented.

Passacaglia: The distinctive characteristic element of this dance is its reiterated descending tetrachordal bass line. Indeed, as with *ostinato* movements in general, this is less a dance form than a vehicle for variations, which determine its tempo.

Passepied: A lively dance similar to the *menuet* but faster, usually notated in $\frac{3}{8}$. There will generally be a hemiola toward the end of the dance, something that does not occur in the *menuet*.

Polonaise: A stately but easily flowing dance with strongly articulated rhythm.

Sarabanda/Sarabande: Seventeenth-century versions of this dance tend to be faster than those of the eighteenth century, but the latter should never be played so slowly as to be un-danceable. There are two distinct types of the dance of this name. The principal characteristic of one is its short-long rhythmic organization within the measure. One should experience the momentum of the quarter-half motion, and then poise a little on the half-note before falling forward again over the bar line into the next short-long figure. The other type moves more serenely but in a tempo that allows the music to flow.[1]

CHAPTER ELEVEN

Ornamentation

Baroque ornamentation can be classified in three categories: symbolic, notated, and spontaneous. I do not propose to provide an exhaustive catalogue but only briefly describe and illustrate those most frequently encountered in violin repertoire.

Symbolic

Symbolic notation of ornaments was most common in French music, but present in all music of the seventeenth and eighteenth centuries. Symbols are, by definition, shorthand, and musical symbols, which varied in meaning from one country or composer to another, were usually translated into real notation in prefatory tables or described in scholarly treatises.

The *gruppo* or *groppo* is usually indicated simply by the word itself, and the speed and duration of the ornament must be based on the context in which it occurs. This forerunner of the main-note trill with a termination may be notated thus:

The *ribattuta* is a type of *gruppo,* a variant that begins with irregular beats of the trilling finger that gradually accelerate into a normal-sounding trill. Still recommended by C. P. E. Bach[1] and Türk[2] at the end of the eighteenth century, this type of trill is therefore appropriate for use in the music of Mozart, Haydn, and Beethoven.

gruppo *ribattuta*

The *trillo,* not to be confused with the trill, is an ornament frequently found in Italian music of the late sixteenth and early seventeenth centuries. Usually indicated by the abbreviation *t* or *tr*, it consisted of the accelerating repetition of a note, usually to a cadence:

t

It can also be a spontaneous ornament, one the performer chooses to add without prompting from the composer. As notated above, it is a typical vocal embellishment but perfectly acceptable for use by a violinist. One may also opt to do something more complex by combining the *ribattuta* and the *trillo,* for example:

The *tremolo,* in turn, is not to be confused with the modern ornament of the same name. In early-seventeenth-century Century violin technique *tremolo* was a kind of right-hand *vibrato,* a pulsation on one pitch in imitation of the "tremulant" organ stop. It is my assumption that the kind of notation found, for example, in the following fragment of the *Sonata Prima a Soprano Solo* by Dario Castello is not to be read literally but is purely symbolic:

It seems to me that one should read this repeated pattern as symbolizing as rapid a pulsation as the tremulant stop on an organ would produce, and therefore not necessarily in slow eighth-notes. As evidence to support this, there is a similar passage in plain half-notes in the bass part of a sonata by Biagio Marini, in which one finds the direction *"metti il tremolo"* ("turn on the tremolo"), which can only be a direction for an organist.

The *appoggiatura* is an ornament that occurs in all Baroque, Classical, and Romantic music. Whereas it may be written out and given full rhythmic value, in Baroque and Classical music it normally appears as a symbol, one that is often misunderstood by performers. Notated as a grace note, its diminutive size belies its importance and potential duration. Derived from the Italian verb *appoggiare,* to "lean upon," its main purpose is to emphasize a dissonant harmony, and there are five types: the variable, the invariable, the superior, the inferior, and the compound.

Variable *appoggiature* are so called because their length depends on context. They may be twice or more as long as the main note. Look, for example, at this moment in Bach's G-minor *Adagio:*

Here the grace note should have the value of a sixteenth-note in order to give the *appoggiatura* its full expressive weight, so that the passage will sound thus:

In this passage from Mozart's E-minor *Sonata*, the quarter-note *appoggiatura* may be played either as a quarter-note or as a half-note.

Its effect as a quarter-note is more lively and as a half-note, more lyrical, and so it could be interpreted in either of the following ways:

To be played thus:

"Invariable" *appoggiature* are played on the beat but with no discernable value, crushed against the main note. Most commonly found in fast movements, their function is to give energetic inflection, as with the opening note of the *allegro* of Mozart's *Fourth Concerto*:

Superior *appoggiature* are simply those that come from above the main note, and inferior *appoggiature* from below. They are often interchangeable and are appropriate in either form, although the use of an inferior one can make the melodic line smoother. Here is such a passage:

Compound *appoggiature* are comprised of more than one note. Played on the beat, at a speed appropriate to the context, they may even have a dotted rhythm, as in this example by Leopold Mozart, which should be played in a fairly lively tempo:

THE TRILL FAMILY

Trills may be played in various ways: brief, long, continuous, and with or without termination. For the correct execution of any trill, however, it is essential to calculate precisely the number of notes it comprises, and to practice it slowly, lifting the trilling finger as high as possible so as to articulate clearly in performance.

The "upper-note" trill is most commonly associated with late-Baroque and Classical repertoire. Think of this trill as a series of *appoggiature*. There is a range of possible executions depending on the tempo of the passage and context in which it occurs. At one end of the range it may begin with a notated *appoggiatura*—or with a note that lingers slightly to draw attention to the dissonance—and then gradually accelerate. This would be appropriate in a slower context, but in an *allegro* a faster execution is necessary. As the first note of a short or rapid trill it should be played crisply to provide clear accentuation.

In the example from Mozart's E-minor *Sonata*, the trill should have a two-note termination, or *Nachschlag:*

The "main-note" trill is related to the *gruppo*. I prefer to describe it as a trill that starts "after the note," and it should always be used when the melody note is dissonant with the bass, as in this example from the *Largo* of Bach's C-major *Solo Sonata*:

In this excerpt it is appropriate to play either a brief main-note trill (without termination, because of the anticipated A) or, perhaps, a *Pralltriller*, since the melodic note is dissonant with the bass. Main-note trills are also generally applicable in late-seventeenth-century German repertoire, and may be performed with or without termination according to context.

The *Pralltriller*[3] is a short trill—only one finger-beat—played upward from the main note, principally in fast passages where there is no time for an upper-note trill:

Leclair's "+": The only symbol used by Jean-Marie Leclair to indicate trill-like ornaments was a cross above the note to be embellished. It may therefore be interpreted in a variety of ways according to the length of the main note, the tempo of the passage, and the affect of the movement. Here is the opening of his D-major *Sonata,* op. 9, no. 3:

Each of the crosses in this excerpt may be interpreted as a short upper-note trill, but there could certainly be justification in other contexts for its interpretation as a *mordant.*

The name of the ornament, *mordent* or *mordant,* is derived from the Italian *mordere,* "to bite," and its function is to accentuate the note on which it occurs to a greater or lesser degree according to its position in a phrase. It is played crisply on the beat with a single swift raising and lowering of the finger and a slight bow accent. The following passage from the *Fourth Concert Royal* by François Couperin has *mordants* on the downbeats of the first and third measures:

The ornament on the downbeat of the second bar is a *port de voix et pincé,* and the one on the fourth is a "tied-over" trill, which, because of the suspended upper note, is played in such a way that the trill commences slightly after the beat. Those on the third quarter-note of the second and fourth bars are short upper-note trills. In this case the grace notes leading to the A in the third bar may be played quickly and lightly before the beat so as to emphasize the A's dissonance with the bass D-sharp.

The *mordente* is an Italianate version of the French-style *mordant,* executed in the same way but with more finger-beats. In the Amsterdam edition of Vivaldi's *Spring* the first bar of birdcalls has an "m" over each quarter-note, which may be interpreted thus:

The *port de voix et pincé,* a quintessentially French compound ornament, is comprised of an inferior *appoggiatura* tied to a *mordent* on the resolution:

Notated Ornaments

Early examples of these are to be found in music composed by seventeenth-century Italians and are used to fill in intervals or elaborate on simple melodic lines. Late sixteenth-century composers for the viola da gamba, such as dalla Casa and Ortiz, had written virtuoso divisions for their instrument, and Italian composers of music for treble instruments were quick to adopt the new melismatic vocal style that reflected the established practice of spontaneous improvised ornamentation. Such writing is also seen in music by German composers in the second half of the seventeenth century, including Schmelzer, Biber, and J. J. Walther.

It is important, therefore, when playing such passages, to give the impression that one is improvising. Here is an early example of a typical melismatic cadential figure, taken from Dario Castello's *Sonata Seconda a Soprano Solo*. The upper line represents the basic melody and the lower, Castello's ornamented version:

When playing *melismata* one should feel as though one is gliding or coasting, by all means shaping the line dynamically according to the *tessitura* and the harmonic tension, but not thinking rhythmically, neither beating time nor counting. In my teaching I liken that sensation to the flight of a frisbee—once it is thrown, the momentum carries it onward without further assistance from the thrower.

These melismatic *passaggi* can be very elaborate, but it is essential to maintain this effortless sense of motion, as though playing only the basic melodic line. Here is a passage from Farina's *Sonata "La desperata,"* as notated in the original, without beams or bar lines:

Here the lower line represents the basic melody. The trill ornament most effective in this context would be a *ribattuta*.

The *Schleifer:* Played on the beat, this ornament should be executed very swiftly, without rhythmic value, as it functions as an accent. It occurs in music from the seventeenth to the nineteenth century. Here is an example from Beethoven's *Quartet in F Major*, op. 135:

Acciaccatura is the name given to an invariable *appoggiatura* so short as to be "crushed" onto the note it precedes. It can be placed above or below the main note and, if it involves string-crossing, may be played almost as a double-stop. Here is a famous passage that is usually misinterpreted, the grace notes played before the beat, making the passage sound ponderous:

The grace notes are *acciaccature* which must be placed on the beat, so that on the third and fourth measures the grace note coincides with the chord in the orchestra.

The *tierce coulée* is an ornament that looks like an *appoggiatura*, but which, in the context of French Baroque music, lightens almost to the point of imperceptibility the last note of the figure. It is one of the few ornaments to be played before the beat:

Un-Notated Ornaments

Certain simple ornaments prescribed in treatises such as *Le nuove musiche* have no symbol, nor will one find their name in any score. These un-notated ornaments, when added spontaneously by the performer, serve to inflect and enliven the interpretation. Anything added to the music by a performer in effect constitutes ornamentation, whether it be notes, articulations, dynamics, accents, or any type of expression. Here are some of the more common un-notated devices:

The *messa di voce* is a commonly used vocal ornament consisting of a swell that may be executed in various ways, such as a quicker *crescendo* or a slower *diminuendo*, depending on the desired effect. Its purpose is to enliven a long note. The opening note of Dario Castello's *Sonata Prima a Soprano Solo* may be played this way. Note also how the notation of the second measure echoes the *messa di voce*.

The *esclamazione* is a device used to treat a long note with dramatic emphasis:

This opening statement of the *Sonata Quarta a sonar con due corde* in Biagio Marini's op. 8 set[4] is a rhetorical outburst, and the dynamics I have suggested are calculated to achieve that effect. Each of the *sfp crescendi* is an *esclamazione,* an ornament described by Caccini in *Le nuove musiche.* Lombardic rhythms, such as the figures that follow them, should always be accentuated in this way.

"*Affetti*" are called for by the composer later in the sonata in the following curious passage:

Affetti

In this context the term is vague, but possibly suggests the addition of connecting notes such as the following:[5]

I do not share the view that the term is synonymous with *tremolo,* as some have suggested, for Marini does use that word in other contexts.

Vibrato is an ornament that may be added either by the left or the right hand. Right-hand *vibrato* may be used as an intensifying ornament. There is a notated instance in Bach's A-minor *Grave:*

In this case, the intention seems to be a *crescendo* intensified by the use of a pulsation of the bow that is achieved by pressure and release of the index finger. The pulsation can accelerate gradually in order to enhance the effect, culminating in a *ribattuta* on the final quarter-note. It is best to continue the *crescendo* through the whole-note in order to make an effective bridge into the *fuga.*

From the outset of the Early Music movement *vibrato* has been a contentious issue, owing in part to recordings in which little or none was used, provoking a backlash from modern players for whom *vibrato* is an essential element of tone production. In modern string playing, of course, *non-vibrato* is a special effect, one a composer requests to create a somber or stark mood. Today constant vibrato is regarded as such a vital component of string technique that we work hard to perfect it and to learn how to vibrate seamlessly between one note and another. It is so identified with tone production that often, if a student is asked to stop vibrating, the bow slows down as well!

This seems to show how modern string players tend to regard the left hand as part of the tone production mechanism rather than that part of the machine whose principal function is simply to change the pitch of the notes. Generally, apart from the use of *portamento* and *glissando*, there is little that the fingers of the left hand do that can be regarded as truly expressive, and, certainly, for those wishing to emulate musicians who lived before the era of constant *vibrato*, the purpose of *vibrato* is secondary—to support the bow in its role as the primary expressive tool by enhancing and reinforcing the expression imparted to the music in the imaginative use of the right hand.

Continuous left-hand *vibrato*, as used by modern performers, was virtually unknown until the third decade of the twentieth century. Leopold Auer,[6] in 1921, complained that some of his students had started doing this, and criticized

> *violinists who habitually make use of the device—those who are convinced that an eternal* vibrato *is the secret of soulful playing, of piquancy in performance . . . Their musical taste . . . does not tell them that they can reduce a programme to the same dead level of monotony by peppering them all with the Tabasco of a continuous* vibrato*. No, the vibrato is an effect, an embellishment; it can lend a touch of divine pathos to the climax of a phrase or the course of a passage, but only if the player has cultivated a delicate sense of proportion in the use of it.*

References to the use of *vibrato* in violin playing occur already in the seventeenth century[7] and in treatises throughout its history. However, until violinists started using it as an element of tone production it was simply regarded as an ornament, to be used sparingly, on appropriate notes and for particular effects.

Geminiani devotes a considerable amount of time to this subject, which he calls the "Close Shake."[8] Here are his words:

> *This cannot be described by Notes . . . when it is long continued swelling the Sound by Degrees, drawing the bow nearer to the Bridge, and ending it very strong it may express Majesty, Dignity, etc. But making it shorter, lower,[9] and softer, it may denote Affliction, Fear, etc., and when it is made on short Notes, it only contributes to make their sound more agreeable and for this Reason[10] it should be made use of as often as possible.*[11]

Therefore, if you wish to play Baroque, Classical, and much Romantic music in a stylistically authentic manner, it is desirable to use *vibrato* strictly as an ornament. As I have remarked earlier, the bow is the primary expressive tool, and when interpreting a phrase, one should first use the bow to shape the musical line with dynamics and tone color, adding *vibrato* to highlight particular notes or to give warmth to an otherwise nasal-sounding one, as, for example, in a *messa di voce*.

I draw your attention, then, to part 2 of this volume, "Left-Hand Technique," where I describe "vertical" *vibrato*, by which the pitch of the note is only subtly altered but produces a warm color. The kind of pitch fluctuation that results from modern-style wrist or arm *vibrato* only weakens the melodic line in Baroque and Classical repertoire, and is particularly inappropriate and distracting in ensemble playing. Note, however, that performers in the Romantic era were also in the habit of using *vibrato* only on particular notes for expressive purposes.

CHAPTER TWELVE

Baroque Clichés

The Classic Cadential Formula

The literature of Baroque music contains certain melodic and rhythmic patterns whose occurrence is so frequent that they are considered to be clichés. I devote this chapter to revealing several of them, with correct and incorrect ways of interpreting them. Here is one of the most common:

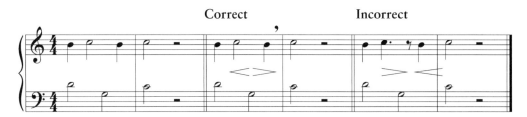

In this example the suspended C becomes a dissonance on the third quarter that then resolves on the B. It is therefore incorrect to make a *diminuendo* on that note, and certainly not a rest, which transforms the B into a pickup to the C. It is best to lift the bow slightly on the bar-line. Try fitting the words "I'm going home" to the melodic line: this phrase exemplifies the articulation appropriate to such a figure.

Slurred Articulations

When playing groups of slurred notes it is important to respect the Baroque and Classical convention according to which the slur infers a *diminuendo*. When two, three, or four notes are slurred there will always be a *diminuendo*. Thus:

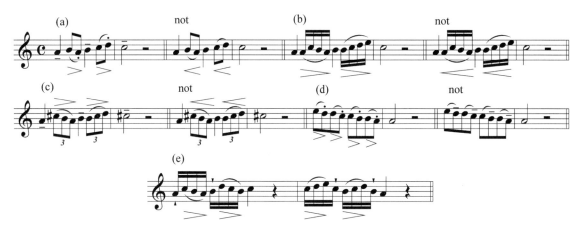

Pairs of slurred, leaping sixteenth-notes are among the most common:

The Hemiola

This is a device that often occurs in movements in triple metre as a means of relaxing the tempo in preparation for the final cadence. Two bars of the basic metre are combined to produce one in which the basic unit is twice as long. Hence, for example, in a *passepied,* two bars of the $\frac{3}{8}$ metre become one in $\frac{3}{4}$. In a $\frac{12}{8}$ it can be a substitute for half a measure, as in this excerpt from Telemann's *Die Kleine Kammermusik:*

In this instance Telemann has inserted the hemiolas as a delaying tactic—effectively two measures in $\frac{3}{4}$—thus paving the way to a more melodically elaborate version of the cadence.

Bach used it in this way in his E-major *Preludio* for solo violin:

Because he has created the effect of a measure in $\frac{3}{2}$, it is important that the down-beat of the second bar (the sixth measure of the example) not be accented, nor the F-sharp/B double-stop. An appropriate bowing, then, would be:

Pulsations

I use this word to describe the way of playing passages such as the following, which will be essentially similar to one another in terms of articulation depending on the contextual affect:

Staccato dots under a slur in Baroque music do not have the same meaning as they might in Romantic violin music, and the appropriate technique ("*portato*") does not involve dry, stopped bow strokes but, rather, constant motion of the arm while pressing and releasing the bow with the index finger to create the pulsations.

Suspensions

The suspension, whereby a note is tied over to the next subdivision of the bar, is a device with an important harmonic function, one much used by Baroque composers to heighten melodic tension. The following passage from a sonata attributed to Handel (op.1, no.10, of doubtful authenticity) contains several suspensions:

Two examples of common errors in the interpretation of these ties follow:

These two versions are illustrations of what happens when the bow is drawn too quickly (the "violin-thing"). In such a situation, frequently found in *adagios,* the sixteenth-note to which the quarter is tied is harmonically stronger and must be sustained and played firmly against the bass note. The following interpretation, in which the tied notes grow dynamically toward the suspension, is stylistically normal:

Syncopations

One exception to the rule stated above is seen in fast movements when a chain of syncopated dissonances and resolutions occurs, as in this passage from a Telemann trio sonata for violin and viola da gamba:

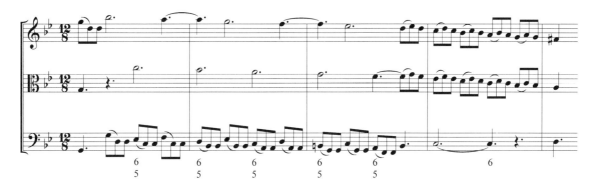

The syncope is an anticipation of a beat and, as such, the note should be treated as though it were actually on the beat. In passages such as this the long notes, both syncopes and those on the main beats, should be lightly accented and decayed in order to preserve the liveliness of the affect:

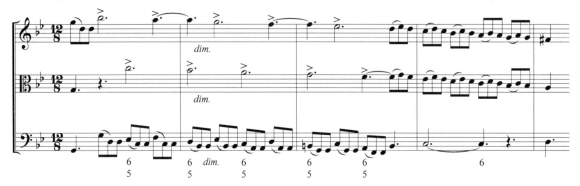

Melodic Accents

Besides syncopes, composers made frequent use of accents created by placing notes of shorter value on a beat followed by longer—a kind of written-out *Schleiffer*—as in this theme from Handel's D-major *Sonata*:

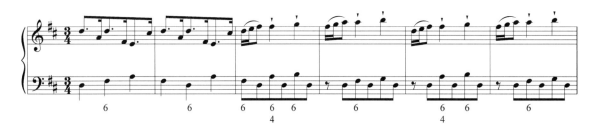

In order to project the energy of this gesture effectively, one must accent the first sixteenth-note and decay rapidly, lifting the bow before the quarter-note:

Notice that the same effect is used by Telemann in the *Kleine Kammermusik* excerpt.

"Down-downs"

In brisk, *vivace* passages, such as the following excerpt from a sonata by Francesco Maria Veracini, a particularly energetic accentuation of the downbeat is achieved by a syncopated rhythmic device popular with Baroque composers:

An appropriate bow-stroke for this figure, in which an equal stress is given to each note, is "down-down":

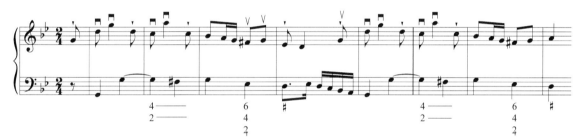

Note that there should be a clear articulation each time between the quarter-note and the pick-up eighth-note and that the eighth-note on the downbeat of measure 4 should be played with a lifted stroke.

The Ultimate Baroque Cliché

The following figure is used more frequently, perhaps, than any of the others I have illustrated. The function of the sixteenth-notes is to lead elegantly from the dissonant fourth or seventh to its resolution, and they should never be given an energetic impulse by lifting or stopping the bow after the suspended eighth-note, nor should they be played with consecutive up-bows. Lightly articulate between the eighth-notes:

The first subject of Bach's G-minor *Fuga* provides a familiar example of this quintessentially Baroque rhythmic motif, and should be bowed "as it comes":

Part 4.

A Technique and Intonation
Practice Guide

CHAPTER THIRTEEN

Tuning

A Word about Intonation

Intonation is certainly one of the more contentious and complex issues in music-making. Over the centuries theorists have wrestled with the problem of the distribution of the "comma"—the amount by which the octave is exceeded when one tunes only in perfect thirds and fifths. In order to arrive at a pure octave, the comma must be divided into small parts that are subtracted from various intervals within it. A number of different solutions, so-called temperaments, were arrived at in the seventeenth and eighteenth centuries, which made some keys more tolerable than others, but as composers experimented with increasingly chromatic keys the subdivision of the comma became, of necessity, more and more equal. In equal temperament, the modern solution to the problem, in which the comma is divided into twelve equal parts, no interval other than the octave is pure.

For string players there are two types of intonation: vertical and horizontal. The latter is often referred to as "expressive" intonation, in which sharps are raised and flats lowered in order to produce a particular expressive effect, and is commonly used in solo performance. When playing in a string quartet or orchestra, however, it becomes immediately apparent that this kind of intonation does not work, and it is in these contexts that familiarity with "vertical" intonation, by which thirds and sixths in a chord are pure, is essential. One should first become familiar with vertical intonation in order to understand that when using "expressive" intonation one is playing deliberately, if creatively, out of tune.

Because of the comma it is impossible to tune a violin so that all intervals are pure. One has to choose between tuning perfect fifths, by which method the ninths (G–A and D–E) and the sixth (G–E) are too wide, or tuning in narrow fifths as described below. When one plays with a harpsichord, each string should be tuned separately in order to match the particular historic temperament (which will virtually never be equal). The tuning system proposed below produces narrow fifths between the open strings but a temperament in which it is possible to tune any note on the instrument to any open string. Using this method you will quickly learn the difference between enharmonic notes: D-sharp, you will find, is lower than E-flat; B-flat higher than A-sharp. You will find that F to F-sharp is a narrow semitone, and F to G-flat is wide. A simple rule, therefore, is that chromatic intervals using the same letter name are narrow and those with different names, wide. In principle, therefore, it is better to use the same finger when playing a narrow semitone and two fingers for a wide one.

I should point out, of course, that in ensemble tuning one should always take the pitch of each open string from the keyboard, which will be in a particular temperament according to the repertoire to be rehearsed or performed. This will probably result in your instrument being tuned differently from what I have described above, but these intonation exercises have the object of training the ear as well as making the left hand secure, so that it should not be a problem for you to adapt to any temperament.

Tuning

The following method of tuning should be used for the intonation exercises:

First make sure by using one of the following chords that the outer strings (E and G) form a perfect sixth:

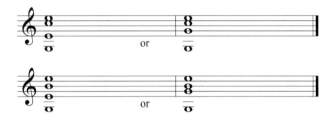

You can then adjust the tuning of the open strings using the following method:
    First, tune the A-string from the G-string:

(Tune the E to the G as a perfect sixth, and then the A to the E.)
    Next, tune the D-string from the E-string:

(Tune the B to the E, and then the D to the B as a perfect sixth.)
    Now the violin is in tune with itself: you'll note, however, that the open-string fifths are narrow.

Difference Tones

A useful tool in verifying the purity of intervals is the so-called difference tone. This is a note created naturally by the subtraction of the frequency of the lower note in a double-stop from that of the upper. It is audible to many people and is, indeed, a device used in modern compositions for flute or horn, wherein the player plays one note and sings another, thereby creating a triad. For string players it is an excellent tool for making sure that a double-stop is in tune.

Here is an interesting passage from Leopold Mozart's *Gründlichen Violinschule:*[1]

In concluding this chapter, I must insert yet another useful observation, of which a violinist can make use in playing double-stops, and which will help him to play with good tone, strongly, and in tune. It is irrefutable that a string, when struck or bowed, sets in motion another string tuned in unison with it. This however, is not enough. I have proved that on the violin, when playing two notes simultaneously, the third, now the fifth, now even the octave, and so on, make themselves heard of their own accord in addition thereto and on the same instrument. This serves then as undeniable proof, which everyone can test for himself, if he be able to play the notes in tune and correctly. For if two notes . . . be so to speak drawn well and rightly out of the violin, one will be able at the same moment to hear the lower voice quite clearly, but as a muffled and droning sound. If on the contrary the notes be played out of tune, and one or the other be stopped even in the slightest degree too high or too low, then will the lower voice be false. Try it patiently, and he who cannot succeed at all therein, let him begin by playing also the black fundamental note and hold the violin nearer to the ear; then will he, while playing the two upper notes, hear this lower black note droning in addition. The nearer the violin is held to the ear, the more the stroke may be moderated. But above all, the violin must be well strung and well tuned. Here are a few proofs thereof. It can be seen herefrom how powerful is the harmonic triad (trias harmonica).

Use difference tones to check intonation while practicing the exercises. Notes may be checked with open strings—even remote ones—in very few steps. For example, for E-sharp on the D-string, form a perfect minor between the C-sharp and open E, then a perfect minor sixth between the C-sharp and E-sharp. Next, to appreciate the enharmonic difference between E-sharp and F-natural, play each with open A. Similarly, to tune D-flat, first tune F perfectly with the A-string and from that find the D-flat.

Here are the most easily heard difference tones:

Minor Third—When played in tune, this produces a difference tone a major third below the lower note. Sometimes the resultant tone will sound an octave lower.

Major Third—When pure, this produces a difference tone an octave below the lower note.

Perfect Fourth—When in tune, this produces a difference tone a fifth below the lower note.

Augmented Fourth—When played in tune, this produces a difference tone a minor tenth below the lower note.

Minor Sixth—When played in tune, this produces a difference tone a major third below the lower note. Sometimes the resultant tone will sound an octave lower.

Major Sixth—When pure, this produces a difference tone a fifth below the lower note.

Difference Tone Exercise

Listen carefully to each difference tone while playing this exercise and remember to keep as many fingers down as possible. Transpose to lower strings as well.

Visualizing

An effective tool in practicing the following exercises, especially where position changes occur, is the "visualization" of each note before you actually play it. The most effective way to use these exercises is to memorize the patterns in order to be able to focus your attention on the sensation of fingering and changing from one position to another, watching neither left hand nor music. There is no point in watching your left hand, which both distracts you from the crucial awareness of the motion of your left arm and causes tension in the neck and shoulder muscles.

When playing the pre-chinrest violin it is essential that the left shoulder not be in contact with the back of the instrument, for doing so has the effect of hampering the vibration and muting the sound. To help achieve this I recommend that you practice the exercises sitting down, so that you are facing directly ahead, both shoulders relaxed, and the instrument at an angle of approximately 30° to the left. In order to "visualize"—to imagine the new position of arm, hand, and fingers before a shift—practice either in a darkened room or with eyes closed, so as not to be distracted. Before starting, spend a few moments breathing deeply from the diaphragm, which will calm your mind and relax your body.

Remember: patience, not speed, is the key to practicing for intonation. Whereas it is inadvisable to practice the exercises too slowly, for that can lead to tension and fatigue, take time whenever necessary to check the intonation of single notes against open strings and to listen carefully for the difference tones.

Warm-Up Exercises

To derive the most benefit from these exercises it is essential to produce as full a sound as possible without forcing, pushing and pulling the bow across the strings and using the weight of the arm, with the elbow and shoulders low. Be sure to hold the first finger down and drop all three of the others simultaneously as you move from string to string. Swing the arm to shift to each new position:

To practice this exercise[2] correctly, it is essential to drop the second, third, and fourth fingers simultaneously, and to sustain the first finger on two strings whenever possible:

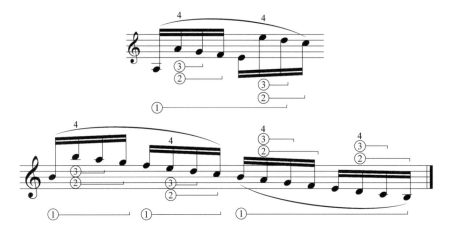

Here is another warm-up exercise from Dounis's *Daily Dozen* that I find particularly effective, especially when following the regimen he prescribed—a theme and six variants: a new one for each day of the week. When changing position be sure to focus on swinging the left elbow, forearm, and wrist in anticipation of the shift. Once you know the notes, play the exercise from memory, facing forward with eyes closed, violin "floating," the left hand as relaxed as possible.[3]

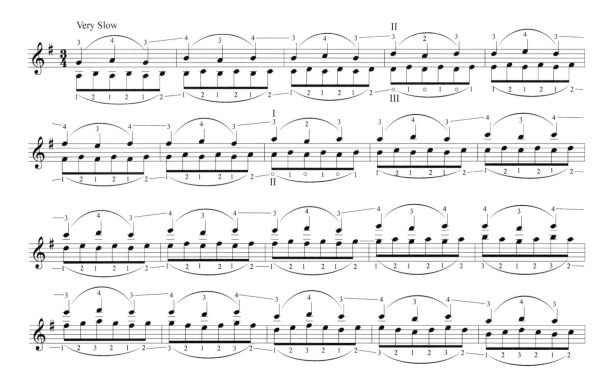

SIX VARIANTS
To be practised one a day,
FOR DEVELOPING THE RYTHM AND THE TRILL-VERTICAL MOVEMENT

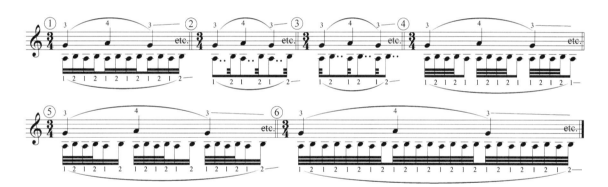

A Shifting Exercise

Here is an exercise based on the shifting patterns on the first page of Geminiani's *Art of Playing on the Violin*. Start each measure with as many fingers down as possible on actual notes, and, keeping them curved, raise and lower them crisply. Never extend—here again, use the same swinging technique to change position and strings.

Exercises Starting with the First Finger

Scales

Use the first finger as the "guiding finger," keeping it down as long as possible. Play the exercise *legato*, varying the number of notes under a slur but usually no more than four and at a moderate tempo, slurring over position changes and string crossings so as not to lose contact with the instrument. Avoid the use of open strings.

Major

Melodic Minor

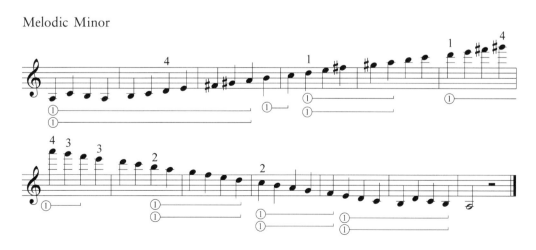

Harmonic Minor

Broken Thirds

Practice, four notes to a bow, slurring across the position changes. When playing broken thirds it is essential to drop the intermediate (silent) finger simultaneously with the sounding one on a real note, and to be sure to keep all fingers down until the next change of position. In the descending shifts and string crossings, be sure to drop all the fingers on the notes they are about to play. As you go through the keys, you will find it useful to start as low as possible (in C, for instance, start on A). Vary position changes, sometimes shifting between third and first, sometimes fifth and third.

Major

Melodic Minor

Harmonic Minor

Double-Stopped Thirds

In this exercise focus on the lower notes, which are melodic, sustaining them throughout the exercise. Here again, slur over the position changes. At the moment of the shift, relax the left hand and use as much weight of the right arm as possible without forcing the sound. Enjoy the sensation of sliding from position to position, and of swinging the left arm to make it happen! As with the exercise in broken thirds, when descending be sure to drop all the fingers simultaneously on the next group of notes, being especially aware of the function of the first as the "guiding" finger.

Major

Melodic Minor

Harmonic Minor

Sixths

These are similar to those in thirds and the same comments apply. The bottom notes are melodic and are to be sustained. Vary the point at which you cross to the next pair of strings.

Major

Alternative Ascending Fingering

Melodic Minor

Harmonic Minor

Octaves

In this set, three different fingerings should be used, changing for each of the modes; it matters not which is used for which, and the choice is best varied. What does matter is that when returning from the sixth to the octave all the fingers fall simultaneously on real notes, and, when using fingering pattern #1, that the third finger be kept down, only the second lifting. When playing the descending octaves, slide lightly, with relaxed fingers, but use the weight of the right arm to keep the bow firmly on the strings. Above all, do not move the thumb with the fingers when sliding. Vary the point at which you change strings, sometimes shifting from third to first position, sometimes fifth to third.

Three Different Fingerings

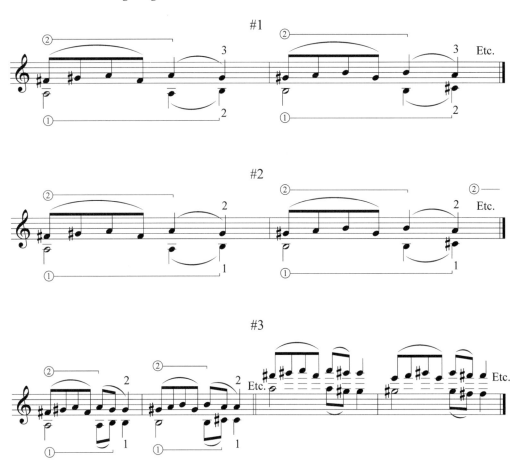

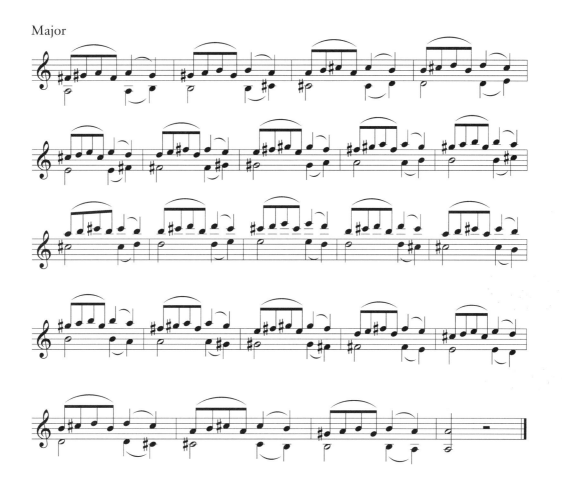

Major

Melodic Minor

Harmonic Minor

Fingered Octaves

Here the top line is melodic, and it is necessary to balance the hand on the third and fourth fingers. For example, in the exercises on A, start with the arm in second position and extend the first and second fingers backward: one must never stretch upward to play a fingered octave. Once again, keep the first and third fingers on the string at all times and, when descending, make sure that they arrive on the notes they will be playing.

Major

Melodic Minor

Harmonic Minor

Tenths

When playing tenths, advance the thumb as far as possible throughout. As in the previous exercise, balance the hand on the 3–1 fingered octave, then add the second finger to form a perfect sixth with the third, and finally make another fingered octave, 4–2, removing the second finger to disclose the tenth. The first and third then slide up to renew the process, never leaving the string. In descending, relax the left side of your body when sliding, and use the weight of your right arm. Though you will be sliding in tenths, the third and first fingers should sustain their fingered octave to stabilize the hand. *(If your hand is too small, do not attempt to play this exercise in lower positions!)*

Major

Melodic Minor

Harmonic Minor

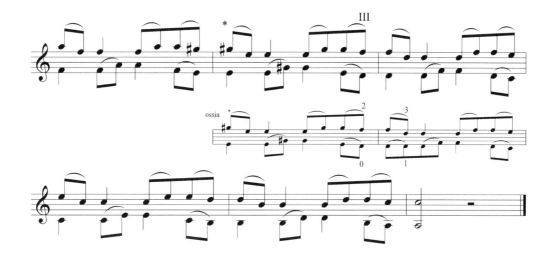

Arpeggios

In these exercises it is important to play as many double-stops as you can. This exercise may be practiced in various ways, and you should vary the number of double-stops. As you climb higher chromatically from C on, start the exercise with the third finger instead of the first. The diminished seventh can be treated enharmonically to include a diminished fifth or an augmented fourth, thereby also providing variety. Be particularly aware of the position-changing function of the left arm throughout, and always drop intermediate fingers on real notes! The exercises can also be played continuously without cadencing each time.

Minor

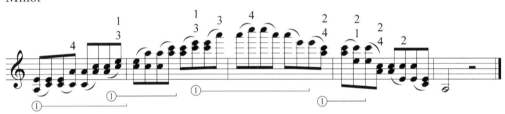

Major

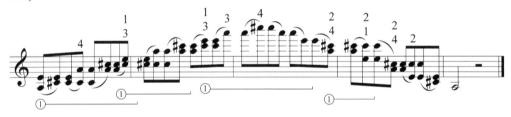

6–3

Major 6–4

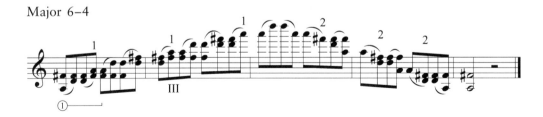

Minor 6–4

Diminished seventh (flats and sharps)

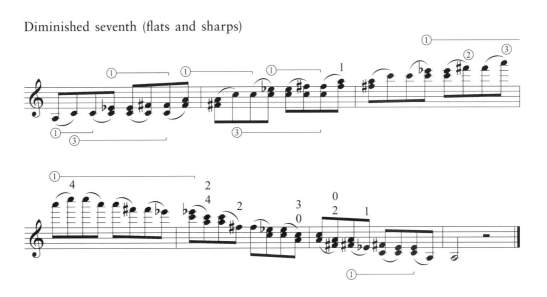

Diminished seventh (sharps)

Diminished seventh (flats)

Dominant seventh

EXERCISES STARTING WITH THE THIRD FINGER

For exercises starting with the third finger, use the following pattern of fingerings and double-stops:

Minor

Major

6–3

Major 6–4

Minor 6–4

Diminished seventh (flats and sharps)

Diminished seventh (flats)

Dominant seventh

CHAPTER FIFTEEN

Exercises Starting on G

Scales

Major

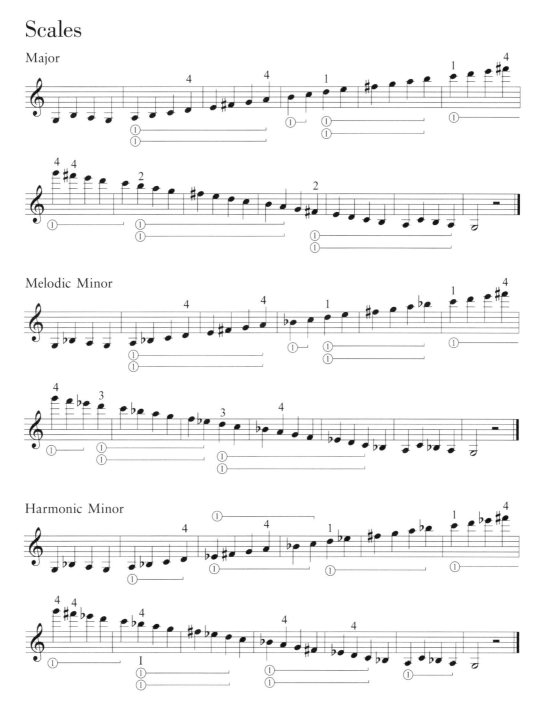

Melodic Minor

Harmonic Minor

Broken Thirds

Major

Melodic Minor

Harmonic Minor

Double-Stopped Thirds

Major

Melodic Minor

Harmonic Minor

Sixths

Major

Melodic Minor

Harmonic Minor

Octaves

Three Different Fingerings

Major

Technique and Practice Guide

Melodic Minor

Harmonic Minor

Fingered Octaves

Major

Melodic Minor

Harmonic Minor

Tenths

Major

Melodic Minor

Harmonic Minor

Arpeggios

Minor

Major

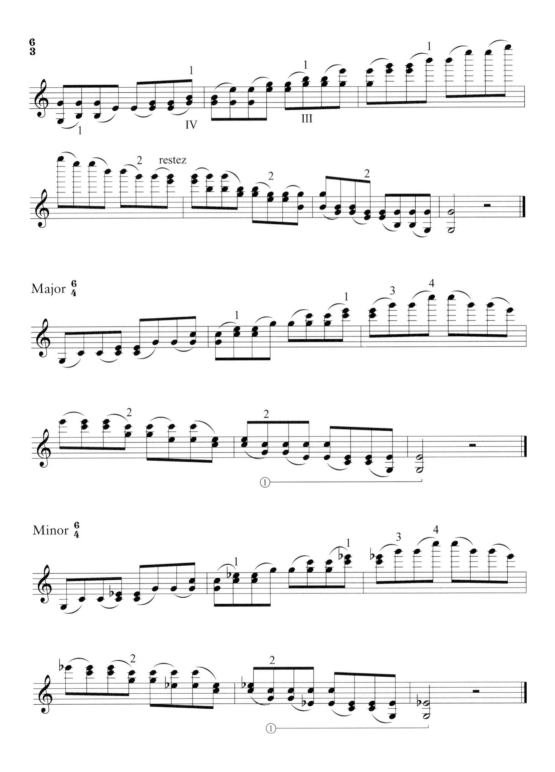

Diminished seventh (flats)

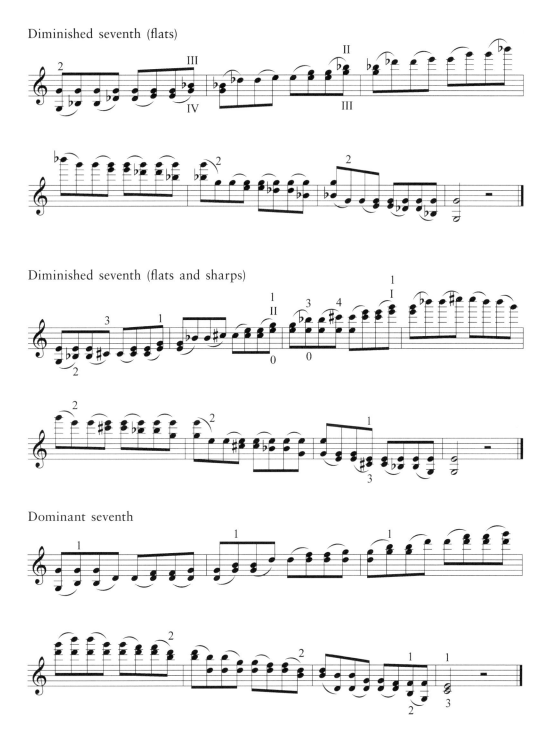

Diminished seventh (flats and sharps)

Dominant seventh

CHAPTER SIXTEEN

Half-Position

When playing the music of Johann Sebastian Bach, one frequently encounters passages such as the excerpt below, from the final chorale of Cantata 138, that require the use of half-position, or at least fall more readily under the fingers when half-position is used. Here, therefore, are some exercises to help you to become more comfortable with its use—the arpeggiated one is but a sample: you should improvise others. Be sure to sustain the fingers on the string for as long as indicated:

In these rapid excerpts from Bach's Cantata 138, it is necessary to change to half-position and then back again. Playing in fourth position is not an option due to the need for tonal clarity.

(a)

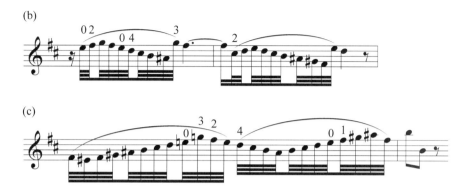

Notes

Introduction

1. It is best to have the instrument fitted with a Baroque-style tailpiece, which is flat, not rounded.

Part 1. Right-Hand Technique

1. The exhaustive bowing exercises in Francesco Geminiani's *The Art of Playing on the Violin* (1751) (Williamstown, Mass.: Broude Bros., PF 238) are much to be recommended.

1. Tone Production

1. The low elbow is a basic tenet of right-arm technique in treatises until the twentieth century.
2. In Geminiani, *The Art of Playing on the Violin*.

2. Bow-Strokes

1. At times, of course, it is necessary to start with the bow on the string, as with a passage of rapid sixteenth-notes after a sixteenth-note rest.
2. Bartolomeo Bismantova, *Compendio musicale* (1677): "*e nel far alle volte de passaggi si suona al punta d'arco con l'arcada corta*" (and at the point of the bow, with short strokes).

3. Chordal Technique

1. In chapter 11 I deal with the manner of executing grace notes such as those in the second and third beat.
2. For an excellent exercise in this technique, see Geminiani, *The Art of Playing on the Violin. Esempio* XVI.

7. Position-Changing Exercises

I refer you also to part 4 of this volume, chapters 13–16, where you will find intonation exercises specifically designed as the continuation of this chapter.
1. This exercise appears in its complete form in chapter 13.
2. For comments on aesthetic considerations concerning vibrato and its appropriate use, see the section titled "Ornaments" in part 3 of the book.

8. Expression

1. Johannes de Grocheio (ca. 1255–ca. 1320).
2. In *Das neu-eroeffnete Orchestre* (1713) and *Der Vollkommene Capellmeister* (1738).
3. Geminiani, *The Art of Playing on the Violin*.
4. In Mary Cyr, *Performing Baroque Music* (Hong Kong: Amadeus, 1992).
5. The literal meaning of the term is "on the breve," a breve having the value of two semibreves (whole-notes) or eight quarter-notes.
6. "*Augmentazione del suono.*"

7. Leopold Mozart, *Versuch einer gründlichen Violinschule,* trans. Editha Knocker (London: Oxford University Press, 1948).

8. Giulio Caccini: *Le Nuove musiche* (1601).

9. It is a common error to change bow here for convenience and play three consecutive eight-note slurs. Bach wrote *articulations, not slurs:* as a violinist he knew what was possible, and at this point he obviously wanted a terraced *crescendo.*

10. One notable exception is to be found in chapter 4 of Michel Corrette's *L'École d'Orphée* (1738).

11. The popular label "double-dotting" should rarely be used for this practice, suggesting as it does a precise mathematical proportion.

12. Mozart, *Versuch einer gründlichen Violinschule.*

13. The "Vega" bow, designed to make it possible to play such chords literally, as they appear and without breaking, is a twentieth-century invention of no proven historical justification.

14. From *Toccate e partite* (1615) *Avertenze al lettore: Primieramente, che non dee questo modo di sonare stare soggetto à battuta, come veggiamo usarsi ne i Madrigali moderni, i quali quantunque difficili si agevolano per mezzo della battuta portandola hor languida, hor veloce, e sostenendola etiandio in aria, secondo i loro affetti, ò senso delle parole* (First of all, this style of playing must not be governed by a [regular] beat but resembles the performance-style of modern madrigals which, however difficult, are easily managed by making the beat sometimes quite slow and sometimes fast, and occasionally even suspending it as it were in mid-air, according to the *affetti* or sense of the words [trans. Christopher Stembridge]).

9. Dynamics and Nuance

1. As, for example, in Michelangelo Rossi's *Toccata Settima.*

2. See his article on temperament in *Groves Dictionary of Music.*

3. See also chapter 8, examples 8.3 and 8.4.

10. Tempo

1. The contrast in style of these types of Sarabande is epitomized by the *sarabandes* in Bach's B-minor and D-minor Partitas, the D-minor *sarabande* characterized by the falling fifth in the melody, which gives a sense of forward motion that is then arrested on the dotted quarter; the B-minor *sarabande* graciously flowing, its serene affect reinforced by the $\frac{9}{8}$ *double.*

11. Ornamentation

1. C. P. E. Bach, *Versuch über die wahre Art das Clavier zu spielen* (1753).

2. Daniel Gottlob Türk, *Clavierschüle* (1789).

3. See also *Mordent.*

4. Biagio Marini, *Sonate, Symphonie . . . a 1–6* (Venice, 1629).

5. See David Boyden, *The History of Violin Playing . . .* (London, 1965), p. 165, ex. 33, quoting Francesco Rognoni, *Selva de varii passaggi secondo l'uso moderno* (Venice, 1620).

6. Leopold Auer, *Violin Playing as I Teach It* (New York, 1921).

7. Marin Mersenne, *Harmonie Universelle* (1636).

8. Geminiani, *The Art of Playing on the Violin.*

9. Probably meaning "further from the bridge."

10. It would seem that Robert Donington (in various writings, including his article on the subject in Grove's *Dictionary of Music*) deliberately omitted the words "and when it is made

on short Notes, it only contributes to make their Sound more agreeable" from this quoted passage in an effort to promote the idea that Geminiani advocated constant *vibrato*. Given that Geminiani is describing here ways of using vibrato to evoke various emotions, I feel that a more accurate interpretation of the word "reason" in this context would be "purpose," referring only to a way of making short notes sound "more agreeable."

11. He goes on to talk at length about bestowing on "Wood and Wire" the "Power of raising and soothing the Passions" and that a master may "by the Help of Variations, Movements, Intervals, and Modulations . . . almost stamp what Impression on the Mind he pleases."

13. Tuning

1. Geminiani, *The Art of Playing on the Violin*.
2. This is an adaptation of an exercise in D. C. Dounis, *The Violin Player's Daily Dozen* (New York: Harms, 1925).
3. This exercise from the Dounis *Daily Dozen* is reproduced as it appears in that publication.

Index

STANLEY RITCHIE, whose career as a modern violinist included the positions of concert master of New York City Opera Orchestra, associate concertmaster at the Metropolitan Opera, and first violinist of the Philadelphia String Quartet, has devoted four decades of his professional life to the study and performance of Early Music. His interest in Baroque violin dates from 1970, and he is internationally recognized as a performer, teacher, and recording artist. A faculty member of Indiana University's Jacobs School of Music since 1982, he has trained two generations of string players in Baroque and Classical style and technique. In 2009 Early Music America honored Ritchie with the Howard Mayer Brown Award for Lifetime Achievement in the Field of Early Music.